CREATIVE CREPE COOKING

Ruth Malinowski and Richard Ahrens

WEATHERVANE
BOOKS

PICTURE CREDITS

The following pictures were provided through the courtesy of Transworld Feature Syndicate, Inc.:

Syndication International: pp. 50 51 52 55 69 79 88 & 89 107 109 127

Scoop: pp.7 8 10 28 47 63 95 97 111 128

Euphot: pp. 34 59 75 92 103 125

Paris Match: pp. 32 41 56 113

Sungravure Syndication: p. 99

Contents

introduction: crepe cookery

The crepe differs from a pancake in that the crepe is thin and delicate and is easily rolled around any filling. The crepe uses eggs instead of baking powder or yeast, as used in pancakes, for leavening. The proportion of liquid to flour is also higher than would be used in making a pancake. Crepes are no harder to make than pancakes, yet lend themselves to an endless variety of interesting dishes from appetizers through desserts.

The use of crepes adds versatility to the repertoire of any cook at the same time it reduces meal preparation time. Crepes freeze superbly and can be prepared ahead. They take up so little space that they can easily be stored in the freezer compartment of a refrigerator-freezer, and they defrost in minutes.

Crepes can make an exotic meal out of leftovers or be the basis of an elegant party dish. As well as their many main-course uses, crepes can be served as hors d'oeuvres or first courses, as vegetable-filled side dishes, and as luscious desserts. Unfortunately, many cooks think of crepes as difficult to make, when the truth is that crepes are easier than pie. The only limit to the great variety of dishes you can make with crepes will be set by your own imagination.

In an age when calorie-counting has become a major preoccupation for many, you will be delighted to know that crepe dishes are light and usually low in calories. The average crepe has only 20 calories and the fillings can be low in calories, too: chicken and mushrooms in a clear delicate sauce, tomatoes and cheese, a vegetable mélange, or a sugarless jam or preserve for a dessert filling.

No special equipment is needed to make crepes. Any small frying pan will work if it is thoroughly cleaned, rinsed and seasoned first. A pan is seasoned by heating it until barely hot to the touch, rubbing it with cooking oil, and letting it stand overnight. Wipe clean with a paper towel and the pan is ready for use.

The most successful crepe pan is made of black iron 5 to 6 inches at the base and with shallow sides to facilitate the turning and tossing of the crepes. Unfortunately, this makes it the perfect size for preparing small quantities of onions, mushrooms, or bacon! Cooking such foods in your crepe pan can have a disastrous effect on the flavor of future crepes. To prevent such disasters, your crepe pan should have a secret hiding place. The pan should be reserved for crepe-making only. If an accident should occur, rub the surface of the pan with a little salt and a few drops of oil to clean it.

technique for making crepes

You can use your pan to make crepes either upside down or right side up. To use it upside down, preheat the pan and dip the bottom into the batter in a 9-inch pie pan. Hold the hot pan bottom in the batter for only a moment. Gently lift the pan up and turn it over. Immediately return the upside down pan to the heat so that the flame or hot element is beneath the inside of the pan. Cook until batter loses its wet look and—with most batters—a very slight browning begins to show on the edge of the crepe. Remove from the heat. Turn the pan over; gently loosen outer edge of the crepe with a thin plastic, wooden, or Teflon®-coated pancake turner or spatula. The crepe should fall onto the stack already cooked. If not, loosen center of the crepe with a spatula.

To use your pan right side up, put about 1 tablespoon of oil in the pan and heat until oil is hot. Tip out the oil. A little will remain clinging to the surface and this will be enough in which to cook the crepes. Return the pan to medium-high heat. With one hand pour in 2 to 3 tablespoons of batter. At the same time lift the pan above the heat source with your other hand. Immediately tilt the pan in all directions, swirling the batter so it covers the bottom of the pan in a very thin layer. Work quickly before the batter cooks too much to swirl. Return to the heating unit and cook over medium-high heat. Cook crepe until bottom is browned. Then carefully turn with a spatula. Brown the other side for a few seconds. Remove from pan with the spatula and add to the stack of already cooked crepes.

The batter should be about the consistency of light cream. If it gets too thick while it is standing, thin the batter by adding more liquid. If the batter becomes too thin, put it into a blender and add more flour.

If the batter forms a clump in the middle of the pan, the pan is too hot. Wave the pan about in the air to cool it down, and lower the heat.

Crepes have an inside and an outside. The side that cooks first is the outside because it looks more attractive. The inside of the crepe is rolled or folded into direct contact with the filling.

common problems in crepe-making

1) Serving crepes inside out: The inside of a crepe is seldom attractive and it detracts from your table setting to stack crepes with the inside most prominent.
2) Serving burned crepes: Displaying burned crepes also detracts from your table setting. Such burning results from extreme heat and excessive cooking time. These crepes were held on high heat too long.
3) Batter too thick: It becomes impossible to coat the bottom of the crepe pan evenly before cooking begins.
4) Pan too hot: The crepe cooks quickly, resulting in lumpiness and gaps.

5) Insufficient batter: The bottom of the crepe pan is not evenly covered with batter, and oddly shaped crepes result.
6) Fragmented crepes: These usually result from insufficient batter in an overheated or improperly seasoned pan.
7) Soggy crepes: These result from prefolding crepes around a juicy or greasy filling too long before serving. It is far better to serve separately a stack of crepes and the filling and permit the diner to fold his or her own.
8) Spongy crepe: Topping a folded crepe with fruit results in the juice being absorbed, leading to dry fruit and a spongy crepe.

Common problems in crepe making:

crepes stacked with insides most prominent

crepes held on high heat too long causing burnt appearance

batter too thick making it impossible to evenly coat the bottom of the crepe pan

pan too hot causing crepe to cook quickly and leading to lumpiness and gaps

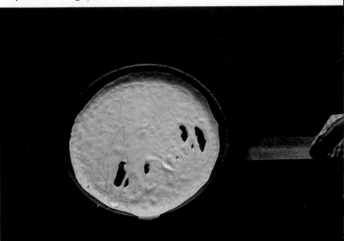

insufficient batter causing bottom of pan not to cover and odd shaped crepes to result

fragmented crepes caused from insufficient batter in an overheated or improperly seasoned pan

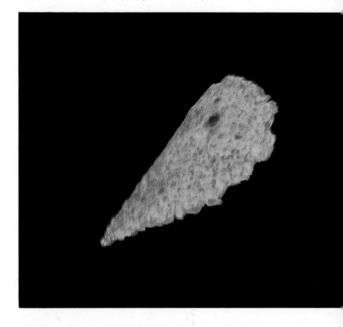

soggy crepes caused by prefolding crepes around a juicy or greasy filling too long before serving

spongy crepes caused by topping a folded crepe with fruit and the juice being absorbed

Some popular ways of serving crepes are:

1) Stack or Gateau: Crepes are stacked with filling between each layer. Place crepes, best side up, on a board or plate. Spread filling over each crepe, leaving about ¼-inch border around edge. Stack one filled crepe on another to desired height. Usually it is easier to spread each one before stacking; but, if filling is runny or hard to handle, you can spread each crepe after it is added to the stack.

2) Crepe Suzette Fold: Place crepe, best-looking side down, on board or plate. Spoon filling on center of crepe. Fold in half. Fold in half again, forming a triangle four layers thick. Excellent for creamy or butter-filled recipes.

3) Blintz or Pocket Fold: Place crepe, best-looking side down, on board or plate. Spoon filling on center of crepe. Fold bottom of crepe over almost half of filling. Fold right side over slightly more than half the filling. Then fold left side of crepe over filling, slightly overlapping right side. Fold top of crepe down over both sides, almost to center. A popular variation of this fold is to fold both sides over filling, then fold bottom and top. This fold keeps the filling inside the crepe—especially good for any recipe to be sautéed or deep-fried.

4) Roll-Up: Place crepe, best-looking side down, on board or plate. Spread filling over other side, leaving about ¼-inch border around edge. Starting at one side, roll up like a jelly roll. This is a good shape for most fillings that can be spread over crepes. Appetizers in this form are easy to cut into bite-size pieces.

5) Fold-Over: Place crepe, best-looking side down, on board, plate, or in pan. Spoon or spread filling along center of crepe. Fold one side over, covering most of the filling. Fold over opposite side, overlapping first fold. This shape is popular because it is easy to make and shows off the filling.

6) Half-Fold: Place crepe, best-looking side down, on board or plate. Place filling on half of the lighter side of the crepe. Fold crepe in half. This is a handy fold for Crepewiches when the filling is too large for other shapes.

7) Burrito Roll: Place crepe, best-looking brown side down, on board or plate. Spread filling over light side, leaving about ½-inch border around edge, or spoon filling into center of crepe. Fold right and left sides over filling. Starting at the bottom of the crepe, roll up. Make sure the folded sides are included in the roll. This is handy for fillings that may become runny when heated. The folded sides help keep the mixture inside the crepe.

some popular ways to serve crepes

10

batter recipes

basic batter

Yield: 24 to 26 crepes
  1½ cups flour
1 teaspoon sugar (for dessert crepes)
⅛ teaspoon salt
3 eggs
1½ cups milk
2 tablespoons butter or oil, melted or cooled

[handwritten: A Little over med. heat.]

[handwritten: med high Little over med]

[handwritten next to milk: 1½ Tbs Less milk]

Sift the dry ingredients into a bowl. Break the eggs into another bowl and mix until yolks and whites are blended. Pour the beaten eggs into a reservoir in the middle of the dry ingredients. (The mixing is more difficult if you break the eggs right into the dry ingredients.)

Stir the flour mixture into the eggs little by little. It may be necessary to add a little milk (or whatever liquid is used in the recipe) to incorporate all the flour. Mix the liquid in thoroughly a spoonful at a time before adding more. When the mixture becomes easy to work (when about half of the liquid has been used), the remainder can be added in two portions.

Add melted butter (and flavorings if indicated). Mix again, cover and set aside for at least an hour but not more than 6 hours at room temperature. Crepe batter can be held overnight in the refrigerator. If necessary, the crepe batter can be cooked immediately, but the "resting" time allows the flour to absorb more liquids, makes the batter easier to handle and gives the crepes more flavor. Since flours vary in their ability to absorb liquid, if the crepe batter seems too thick when you are ready to cook it, a small amount of extra liquid can be added at this time. The consistency should be at least as thin as heavy cream.

Mixer or whisk method: In medium mixing bowl, combine eggs and salt. Gradually add flour, alternating with milk, beating with an electric mixer or whisk until smooth. Beat in melted butter.

Blender method: Combine ingredients in blender jar; blend for about 1 minute. Scrape down sides with rubber spatula and blend for another 15 seconds or until smooth.

richer batter

Yield: 30 to 35 crepes
  4 eggs
  ¼ teaspoon salt
  2 cups flour
  2 cups milk
  ½ cup melted butter

Mixer or whisk method: In medium mixing bowl, combine eggs and salt. Gradually add flour, alternating with milk, beating with electric mixer or whisk until smooth. Beat in melted butter.

Blender method: Combine ingredients in blender jar; blend for about 1 minute. Scrape down sides with rubber spatula and blend for another 15 seconds or until smooth.

This is a thick batter. You may want to add 1 or 2 tablespoons of milk or water for thinner crepes. Refrigerate at least 1 hour before using.

instant flour batter

Yield: 16 to 20 crepes
  3 eggs
  ¼ teaspoon salt
  1 cup instant flour
  ⅔ cup milk
  ⅔ cup water
  1 tablespoon cooking oil

Mixer or whisk method: In medium mixing bowl, combine eggs and salt. Gradually add flour, alternating with milk and water, beating with electric mixer or whisk until smooth. Beat in oil.

Blender method: Combine ingredients in blender jar; blend for about 1 minute. Scrape down sides with rubber spatula and blend for another 15 seconds or until smooth.

This batter does not have to be refrigerated before using. You can use it right away. Be sure to stir batter occasionally, as flour has a tendency to sink.

basic dessert crepe batter

Yield: 20 to 25 crepes
   4 eggs
   1 cup flour
   2 tablespoons sugar
   1 cup milk
   ¼ cup water
   1 tablespoon melted butter

Mixer or whisk method: In medium mixing bowl, beat eggs. Gradually add flour and sugar alternating with milk and water, beating with electric mixer or whisk until smooth. Beat in melted butter.

Blender method: Combine ingredients in blender jar; blend for about 1 minute. Scrape down sides with rubber spatula and blend for another 15 seconds or until smooth.

Refrigerate batter at least 1 hour before use.

chocolate dessert crepe batter

Yield: 18 to 22 crepes
   3 eggs
   1 cup flour
   2 tablespoons sugar
   2 tablespoons cocoa
   1¼ cups buttermilk (or add
      1 tablespoon lemon juice to 1¼
      cups regular milk)
   2 tablespoons melted butter

Mixer or whisk method: In medium mixing bowl, beat eggs. Add flour, sugar, and cocoa, alternating with buttermilk, beating with electric mixer or whisk until smooth. Beat in melted butter.

Blender method: Combine ingredients in blender jar; blend for about 1 minute. Scrape down sides with rubber spatula and blend for another 15 seconds or until smooth.

Refrigerate batter for at least 1 hour before use.

special tips for perfect crepes

1. If batter is lumpy, strain through sieve.
2. Make batter and store in refrigerator up to 3 days. Bring to room temperature before using.
3. Pratice making thinner more delicate crepes by using less batter.
4. Use a small measuring cup to dip up batter when making crepes.
5. Brush spatula with melted butter or oilk to prevent it from sticking to crepes white turning.
6. Makes crepes ahead of time. Stack, wrap, and refrigerate 1 to 2 days. Freeze up to 2 months.
7. If flaming crepes, ignite slightly warm alcohol with a long wooden match. Slowly pour over food.
8. Use high-proof liqueur for flaming.

sauces for crepes

All sauces yield approximately 1 cup.

white sauce

1 tablespoon butter
1 cup flour
1 cup milk

Melt the butter in a small saucepan. Remove from the heat and add the flour, stirring with a wire whisk. Add the milk gradually, stirring the mixture constantly until the sauce has thickened. Season with salt and pepper.

mornay sauce

1 tablespoon butter
1 tablespoon flour
1 cup milk
3 tablespoons grated Swiss or
    Gruyére cheese
1 tablespoon grated Parmesan
    cheese
½ teaspoon mild prepared
    mustard, preferably of the
    Dijon type

Melt the butter in a small saucepan. Remove from the heat and add the flour, stirring with a wire whisk. Return to a moderate heat. Add the milk gradually, stirring the mixture constantly until the sauce is thickened. Add the remaining ingredients, and salt and pepper to taste.

veloute sauce

1 tablespoon butter
1 tablespoon flour
1 cup chicken stock or chicken
    broth

Melt the butter in a small saucepan. Remove from the heat and add the flour, stirring with a wire whisk. Add the chicken stock gradually, stirring constantly over a moderate heat. In order to enrich the sauce and give it a more beautiful color, combine the following:

1 egg yolk
1 to 2 tablespoons whipping cream
Add about 3 tablespoons of the hot sauce into the combined egg yolk and cream and stir together. Return it to the remaining hot sauce. Do not let the sauce boil after the egg yolk and cream have been added.

handmade hollandaise

1¾ sticks of butter
3 egg yolks
1 tablespoon cold water
Juice of 2 lemons
¼ teaspoon salt
Dash cayenne pepper
Melt 1½ sticks of butter. Have 2 separate tablespoons of cold butter on the counter.

In a heavy saucepan, beat the egg yolks with a wire whisk until slightly thickened. Add the water, lemon juice, salt and cayenne pepper. Put the pan on a gentle heat and add the first tablespoon of cold butter. Stir rapidly with a wire whisk. Allow the butter to melt but not completely disappear, then add the second tablespoon of cold butter. When the butter has almost melted, remove the pan from the heat. Gradually add the hot butter, still stirring rapidly and constantly. The egg yolks will combine with the hot butter and thicken off the heat into a beautiful smooth sauce. Check the seasoning, adding more lemon juice or salt if necessary.

blender hollandaise

3 egg yolks
Juice of 1 lemon
Dash cayenne pepper
Pinch of salt
1 stick of butter
Put the egg yolks, lemon juice, cayenne pepper and salt into the blender. Heat the butter until hot and bubbling but not browned.

Turn on the blender and pour in the hot butter in a slow continuous stream. Blend for 10 seconds and turn off the motor. Taste and add more lemon juice or salt to your taste. Serve immediately or reheat by standing the sauce in a basin of hot but not boiling water. This sauce will keep for 2 or 3 days in the refrigerator.
Note: Hollandaise does not need to be boiling hot. The food on which it is served will heat it up a little. By trying to get it as hot as possible the risk of curdling is greatly increased.

tomato sauce

3 medium-size ripe sliced
    tomatoes
½ small onion
1 bay leaf
½ cup chicken stock or chicken
    broth

Simmer the above ingredients for 20 minutes. Put into the blender for 10 seconds and pass through a sieve to remove the tiny pieces of tomato skins.

1 tablespoon butter
1 tablespoon flour
1 cup flavored tomato juices from
    above
1 teaspoon sugar
¼ teaspoon rosemary or ¼
    teaspoon basil or ¼ teaspoon
    oregano
½ teaspoon tomato paste
    (optional)

Melt the butter and add the flour. Add the strained tomato juices gradually, stirring the sauce with a wire whisk until thickened. Add the sugar and herbs and simmer the sauce for 5 minutes. Correct the seasoning with salt and pepper.
Note: It may be necessary to add the optional tomato paste in the winter months when the tomatoes have less flavor. This is an excellent sauce for spaghetti as well as other foods.

marmalade sauce

1 cup orange, lemon or lime
    marmalade
Juice of 1 orange, lemon or lime
Pinch of ground ginger
(1 teaspoon prepared horseradish
    for shrimp or crab crepes)
(¼ teaspoon cloves and ¼ teaspoon
    cinnamon for apricot crepes)

Put the above ingredients in the blender for 10 seconds.

handmade melba sauce

2 cups fresh raspberries or
    strawberries
2 tablespoons water
2 tablespoons sugar
Juice of ½ lemon
1 teaspoon arrowroot
1 tablespoon cold water

Wash berries and place in a small saucepan with the 2 tablespoons water, sugar, and lemon juice. Simmer together gently for 5 minutes and press through a fine sieve. Return to a clean saucepan and thicken with 1 teaspoon arrowroot dissolved in 1 tablespoon cold water. Chill before serving.

blender melba sauce

1 package frozen raspberries
3 tablespoons sugar
Juice of ½ lemon
1 tablespoon Framboise, cognac,
    or kirsch (optional)
1 or 2 teaspoons arrowroot or
    cornstarch (optional)
1 tablespoon cold water (optional)

Defrost the raspberries and place in the blender with the remaining ingredients. Turn on the motor for 10 seconds and pass the liquid through a fine sieve to remove the tiny seeds. This and all fruit sauces may be thickened, if desired, with 1 or 2 teaspoons arrowroot or cornstarch dissolved in 1 tablespoon cold water. Bring the sauce to the boil and add the thickening. It will thicken immediately, leaving no taste.

pineapple sauce

**Juice from a 1-pound 4-ounce can
    crushed pineapple**
1 tablespoon butter
2 whole eggs
1 tablespoon sugar
1 tablespoon cornstarch
¼ teaspoon almond extract
1 tablespoon kirsch

Melt the butter in the pineapple juice. In a separate bowl combine the eggs, 1 tablespoon sugar and 1 tablespoon cornstarch. Pour the boiling pineapple juice into the contents of the bowl and stir over gentle heat until thickened. Remove from the heat and add almond extract and kirsch.

peach sauce

Yield: 4 or more cups
    2 cups water
    1 cup sugar
    2 strips lemon rind
    Juice of ½ lemon
    **6 ripe fresh peaches or ½ pound
        dried peaches soaked
        overnight in water**

Make a syrup by combining the sugar and water. Add the lemon juice and rind. Simmer the peaches in the syrup for 10 minutes. Remove the peaches and press through a sieve or blender, adding a little of the syrup in which the peaches were poached to correct the consistency of the sauce.

chocolate sauce

**6 ounces semisweet chocolate
    pieces**
3 tablespoons cold water
⅓ cup heavy cream
1 tablespoon butter
1 tablespoon dark rum

Melt the chocolate in the water and add the remaining ingredients. Serve hot or cold. The sauce will thicken as it cools and will require reheating and thinning out with a little more cream or water if it is taken right from the refrigerator.

spiced apricot sauce

1 10-ounce jar apricot preserves
Rind and juice of 1 lemon
Pinch of cinnamon
Pinch of cloves
1 teaspoon arrowroot or 1 teaspoon
    cornstarch dissolved in
1 tablespoon cold water

Melt the apricot preserves in a small heavy saucepan, adding the juice and rind of a lemon and the spices. Strain the contents of the pan and return the clear liquid into a clean saucepan. Dissolve the arrowroot or cornstarch in the water and add to the sauce. As the sauce comes to the boiling point, it will thicken. This sauce can be used hot or cold.

Note: Arrowroot is used in preference to cornstarch to make a clearer more shiny sauce. However, if you are not able to find any arrowroot, cornstarch is a good substitute.

lemon sauce

1 cup water
1 tablespoon butter
½ cup sugar
2 whole eggs
Juice of 1 lemon
1 tablespoon cornstarch
1 teaspoon vanilla

Melt the butter in the water with half of the sugar. In a separate bowl combine the eggs and the remaining sugar with the juice of the lemon. Add 1 tablespoon cornstarch.

Pour the boiling water, sugar and melted butter into the eggs, sugar, lemon juice and cornstarch and stir over a gentle heat until thickened. Add 1 teaspoon vanilla.

appetizers

Crepe appetizers may be new to you, but they are an excellent way to get your meal off to the right start. They also make delightful hors d'oeuvres for your next party. They are bite-size so lots of them can be made out of a very few crepes. Crepe appetizers may be served heated or unheated, depending on personal preference. Serve them alone on an appetizer tray or combine on a toothpick with an olive, cherry, tomato, or cocktail onion. Less well-known, but delicious, crepes can be cut into strips and used in place of noodles in clear soup.

chili-blue cheese crepes

Yield: 6 servings (16 to 20 appetizers)

1 ounce crumbled blue cheese
1 3-ounce package cream cheese,
    softened
1 tablespoon catsup
½ teaspoon chili powder
¼ teaspoon paprika
1/16 teaspoon garlic powder
4 crepes

Blend blue cheese and cream cheese with catsup, chili powder, paprika, and garlic powder. Spread over crepes. Broil until cheese bubbles. Roll up each crepe—jelly roll style—and cut each roll into 4 or 5 pieces. Serve immediately.

appetizer wedges

Yield: 8 servings

1 8-ounce package cream cheese,
    softened
2 teaspoons milk
1 tablespoon grated onion
½ teaspoon garlic salt
¼ teaspoon black pepper
½ cup sour cream
⅓ cup bacon bits or 6 strips bacon,
    fried and crumbled
¼ cup finely chopped green
    pepper
12 cooked crepes
½ cup chopped pecans

In a small mixing bowl mix cream cheese with milk, onion, garlic salt, pepper, and sour cream until smooth. Stir in bacon and green pepper. Spread 2 tablespoons cheese mixture over each crepe. Make 2 stacks, each 6 crepes high. Sprinkle tops with chopped pecans. Refrigerate until firm—1 hour or more. Cut into wedges for serving.

cheese-olive snack

Yield: 12 servings (80 to 95 appetizers)
2 cups grated sharp cheddar cheese
15 stuffed green olives, chopped
2 tablespoons finely chopped
    green onions
1 cup mayonnaise
16 crepes
Bacon bits or bacon, cooked and
    crumbled

Combine cheese with olives, onions, and mayonnaise. Spread on crepes. Broil until cheese bubbles. Sprinkle with bacon bits and cut each crepe into 5 or 6 wedges. Serve immediately.

cheese and beef rolls

Yield: 8 to 10 servings (60 appetizers)
½ pound sharp cheddar cheese
1 small onion, chopped
1 2½-ounce package dried beef,
    finely chopped
1 teaspoon dry mustard
½ teaspoon Worcestershire sauce
2 teaspoons mayonnaise
16 crepes
Melted butter

Put cheese and onion through a food grinder or blender (a little at a time). Stir in dried beef, mustard, Worcestershire sauce and mayonnaise. Form into several rolls about ½ inch in diameter and 12 to 14 inches long. Cut each roll into pieces about 4 to 5 inches long. Place one cheese log in center of each cooked crepe. Roll up and refrigerate until just before serving. Place on broiler pan; brush with melted butter. Broil until cheese bubbles. Cut each crepe into 4 or 5 crosswise pieces. Serve warm.

crepes with fillings

Yield: 6 servings
- **1-pound package bacon strips, cut in half**
- **1 pound fresh mushrooms**
- **1 small green pepper**
- **1 small red pepper**
- **12 warm crepes**

Fry bacon until crisp. Drain on paper towels. Wash mushrooms and fry until browned. Clean peppers and cut into strips. Serve with crepes and let guests fill their own.

crepes with fillings

cheesy dipping chips

Yield: 10 servings (72 to 96 dippers)
6 cooked crepes
Melted butter
Grated Parmesan cheese
Brush crepes with butter; sprinkle with grated cheese. Cut each crepe into 12 to 16 wedges. Place on cookie sheet. Bake at 325° for 6 to 9 minutes or until crispy. (Use Italian seasoning or garlic salt for variations.)

smoked oyster crepes

Yield: 4 servings
1 3-ounce package cream cheese,
  softened
2 tablespoons mayonnaise
1 tablespoon finely chopped green
  onions
1 teaspoon finely chopped
  pimiento
1 3½-ounce can smoked oysters,
  drained and chopped
8 cooked crepes
Combine cream cheese with mayonnaise, green onions, pimiento, and oysters. Spread on crepes and roll up. Broil until bubbly and serve hot for first course.

crabby crepes

Yield: 8 to 10 servings (64 wedges)
1 teaspoon chopped chives
⅛ teaspoon tarragon
2 teaspoons chopped parsley
⅛ teaspoon chervil
6 ounces crab meat
1 cup mayonnaise
8 crepes
Combine herbs and crab meat with mayonnaise. Refrigerate for 1 hour to blend flavors. Spread on crepes. Cut each crepe into 8 wedges. Roll up like a crescent roll and serve on toothpicks.

curried crab appetizers

Yield: 6 to 8 servings
- **1 can crab meat, drained**
- **¼ teaspoon salt**
- **½ teaspoon curry powder**
- **3 tablespoons mayonnaise**
- **1 teaspoon lemon juice**
- **1 teaspoon instant minced onion**
- **6 crepes**
- **Paprika**

Shred crab meat and add salt, curry powder, mayonnaise, lemon juice, and onion. Spread on crepes in a thin layer. Roll up and chill. When ready to use, cut each crepe into 3 or 4 pieces. Sprinkle with paprika and serve.

deviled-crab crepes

Yield: 6 to 8 servings
- **2 tablespoons butter**
- **2 tablespoons onion, minced**
- **2 tablespoons green pepper, minced**
- **1 tablespoon celery, minced**
- **2 teaspoons cornstarch**
- **½ cup heavy cream**
- **2 egg yolks**
- **1 teaspoon prepared mustard**
- **½ teaspoon paprika**
- **Salt and pepper to taste**
- **Cayenne if desired**
- **½ pound crab meat, shredded (canned or fresh)**
- **8 warm crepes**

Melt butter and sauté the onions, green pepper, and celery until soft—about 5 minutes. Stir the cornstarch into the cream, add egg yolks and beat well. Add mustard, paprika, salt and pepper and cayenne if desired. Add the crab meat to the vegetables and cook for 1 to 2 minutes over high heat. Reduce heat and add cream-egg yolk mixture, stirring thoroughly. Spread over half the crepes and top with remaining crepes. Place on a greased cookie sheet and bake at 400° for about 20 minutes. Cut into wedges and serve with cocktails.

tuna paté crepes

Yield: 12 servings

1 8-ounce package cream cheese, softened
2 tablespoons chili sauce
2 tablespoons minced parsley
1 chopped green onion
½ teaspoon bottled hot pepper sauce
2 7-ounce cans tuna, drained
12 crepes

Blend cream cheese, chili sauce, parsley, onion, and hot sauce. Add tuna and mix well. Spread on crepes and roll up. Chill until ready to use. Cut each crepe into 3 or 4 pieces. Place a toothpick in each piece and serve.

crepes with caviar

Yield: 4 to 6 servings

8 to 10 Warm crepes
½ cup Red caviar
½ cup Black caviar
8 to 10 Lemon wedges

Have the above foods available and allow guests to make their own delicious crepes. These crepes would be perfect for an informal yet elegant cocktail party.

crepes with caviar

crepes with bacon quiche

Yield: 18 servings

8 ounces cream cheese	2 tablespoons chopped chives
½ cup heavy cream	4 tablespoons Swiss cheese, grated
1 egg	4 strips bacon, cooked and
1 egg yolk	crumbled
⅛ teaspoon black pepper	18 small crepes—about 5 inches

Soften cream cheese at room temperature for 1 hour before starting. Gradually blend in the heavy cream, whole egg, and egg yolk until the mixture is smooth and thick. Add black pepper, chives and grated cheese and mix well.

Bake in 3 muffin tins. Place a crepe over one opening, add a few bits of bacon and a spoonful of cheese mixture in the center. Gently push crepe into muffin cup. Repeat until all crepes are filled. The crepes will act as pastry shells. Bake for 30 minutes in a 375° oven.

crepes with ham quiche

Yield: 18 servings

Follow the directions for bacon quiche. Use ¼ pound leftover ham cut into small cubes, instead of bacon. Place in center of crepes before adding the cheese mixture.

deviled-ham crepes

Yield: 8 servings

2 4½-ounce cans deviled ham
10 chopped stuffed green olives
1 tablespoon prepared mustard
1 3-ounce package cream cheese, softened
2 teaspoons milk
8 crepes

Combine ham, olives, and mustard. Add cream cheese and milk and mix well. Spread on crepes. Place in hot oven (425°) for 3 minutes or until bubbly. Cut into wedges and serve.

dried beef appetizers

Yield: 8 to 10 servings
  **1 8-ounce package cream cheese,
     softened**
  ¼ cup grated Parmesan cheese
  1 tablespoon prepared horseradish
  ⅓ cup stuffed green olives
  **2 to 3 ounces dried beef, finely
     chopped**
  8 crepes
  Stuffed olives for garnish
  Combine cheeses, horseradish, olives, and dried beef. Spread on crepes and
roll up. Chill until ready to serve. Cut each crepe into 3 or 4 pieces. Place on a
toothpick with a stuffed olive and serve.

crepes with chicken-liver paté

Yield: 6 servings
  2 tablespoons butter
  ½ pound chicken livers
  2 eggs, hard-cooked
  **2 packages (3-ounce size) soft
     cream cheese**
  **1 tablespoon finely chopped
     parsley**
  1 teaspoon salt
  ⅛ teaspoon pepper
  1 tablespoon cognac
  12 crepes
  1 tablespoon melted butter
  Heat butter in frying pan. Add chicken livers and cook, stirring occasionally,
over medium heat for 10 minutes or until tender. Drain.
  Chop livers and eggs in a food grinder or blender (add a little at a time). With
spoon, work cream cheese until light and fluffy. Mix cheese into liver mixture along
with all remaining ingredients except melted butter.
  Put 2 spoonfuls along the center of each crepe; roll and turn seam side down in
a buttered baking dish. Brush with melted butter and bake at 375° for 15 to 20
minutes. These may be served hot as a first course or sliced and served cold as an
hors d'oeuvre.

french onion soup with crepes

Prepare favorite onion soup recipe. Instead of toast, use crepes cut into noodle strips. Put the crepe strips on top of soup in individual ovenproof bowl and sprinkle with cheese. Broil for 3 to 4 minutes, until cheese bubbles and browns slightly.

bouillon with crepes

Yield: 6 servings
**4 cups beef bouillon or clarified
    stock
Slivered raw beef or leftover rare
    roast beef (about ¼ pound)
4 crepes
1 tablespoon chopped parsley**

Bring the bouillon to a boil. Add slivered beef and simmer for 1 to 2 minutes. Add the crepes. Cut in strips. Add parsley and serve at once.

chicken consommé with crepes

Yield: 4 servings
**4 cups clarified chicken broth or
    bouillon
1 cup chopped raw chicken (or ¼
    pound)
6 crepes
Watercress for garnish, chopped**

Heat broth or bouillon. Cut chicken into very thin slivers and simmer for 2 or 3 minutes in the liquid. Cut crepes into long thin strips. Add crepes to broth and heat through. Float watercress on top.

spontaneous crepe snacks

There is no need to be confined by a recipe in formulating crepes. Almost any combination of leftovers can make a delicious snack, as shown in the photograph.

Left Crepe—Slice of ham, chopped green olive, mushrooms and sour cream.

Middle Crepe—Sardines mixed sweet pickles, green onion tops sliced very thin lengthwise, and tartar sauce.

Right Crepe—Cottage cheese, walnuts, raisins, chopped green onion tops, and blue-cheese flavoring.

spontaneous crepe snacks

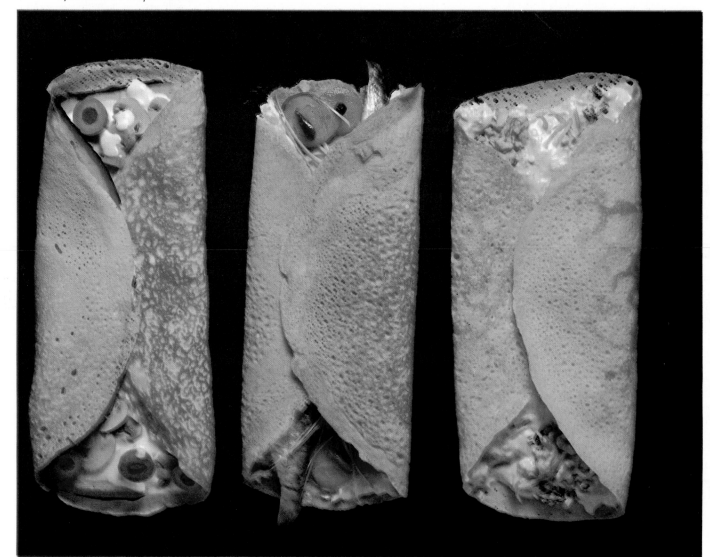

vegetable crepes

Use your imagination for interesting crepe dishes. Suggested fillings include sautéed mushrooms with chopped parsley, sautéed onions with tomatoes and chopped parsley, sautéed peas with asparagus tips or caviar paste, and unflavored yogurt and chives.

egg and zucchini crepes

Yield: 4 to 6 servings

1 cup dry bread crumbs
½ cup butter
⅓ cup minced onion
1 large zucchini, cut into julienne
   strips
3 eggs, lightly beaten
½ teaspoon salt
⅛ teaspoon pepper
3 tablespoons minced parsley
12 crepes
⅓ cup grated Parmesan cheese
⅓ grated Gruyère cheese

Sauté bread crumbs in half the butter, tossing them until lightly toasted. Remove from pan and reserve. Add rest of butter to pan and sauté onion and zucchini until the vegetables are tender. Add the eggs, salt and pepper and with a fork very lightly scramble the mixture over low heat. Add the egg mixture to the bread crumbs. Stir in parsley and divide the mixture between the crepes. Roll up and arrange seam side down in a buttered shallow baking dish. Sprinkle crepes with cheeses and bake at 375° for 10 minutes or until hot and cheese is golden.

crepes madrilene

Yield: 6 servings

1 onion, sliced
1 tablespoon vegetable oil
4 tomatoes, peeled and cut in
   wedges
1 teaspoon dried thyme
1 green pepper, sliced in strips
1 red pepper, sliced in strips
Several pitted black olives
Several pitted green olives
1 clove garlic, crushed
½ teaspoon salt
¼ teaspoon pepper
6 crepes

Heat oil and sauté the onion until soft. Add tomatoes, thyme, peppers, olives, garlic, salt and pepper. Simmer for a few minutes to soften tomatoes and peppers. Spoon over crepes, and garnish.

crepes madrilene

asparagus and egg crepes

Yield: 8 servings
- **2 pounds fresh asparagus**
- **4 eggs, hard-cooked and sliced**
- **8 crepes**
- **½ teaspoon salt**
- **⅛ teaspoon pepper**

hollandaise sauce:

- **3 egg yolks**
- **¼ teaspoon salt**
- **½ teaspoon dry mustard**
- **1 tablespoon lemon juice**
- **½ cup butter**

Cook asparagus in salted water until tender. Drain. Arrange eggs and asparagus on crepes. Season with salt and pepper. Fold crepes and place in a shallow baking dish. Cover with a foil top. Heat at 350° for 10 minutes or until warm.

To make sauce, place yolks, salt, mustard and lemon juice in blender. Cover and blend until eggs are well-mixed. Heat butter until bubbling hot and immediately pour butter in a tiny stream through small opening in top of blender, keeping blender on low until mixture is thickened. Spoon sauce over warm crepes. Serve immediately.

green crepes

Yield: 4 servings
- **Basic crepe batter**
- **½ package frozen chopped spinach**
- **½ teaspoon chervil, crumbled**
- **2 tablespoons chopped chives**

Thaw the spinach. Add spinach, chervil, and chives to batter. Make thin crepes. Serve with a cup of hot bouillon, seasoned if desired with chives.

green beans in cheese crepes

Yield: 6 servings

1 tablespoon butter
1 tablespoon flour
¼ teaspoon salt
1 teaspoon minced onion
⅛ teaspoon pepper
½ teaspoon grated lemon peel
¼ cup water
½ cup dairy sour cream

1 10-ounce package frozen
    French-style green beans,
    cooked and drained
6 crepes
¼ cup grated cheddar cheese
1 tablespoon melted butter
¼ cup dry bread crumbs

In saucepan, melt 1 tablespoon butter and stir in flour, salt, onion, pepper, and lemon peel. Add water and cook over medium heat until thick and bubbly. Stir in sour cream and green beans. Divide mixture between crepes; fold over. Mix cheese with melted butter and bread crumbs. Sprinkle over filled crepes. Broil until cheese melts.

green crepes

ratatouille crepes

Yield: 4 servings
  2 tablespoons olive oil
  1 onion, finely chopped
  1 clove garlic, crushed
  1 green pepper, chopped
  1 zucchini or 1 cucumber, diced
  **3 slices of eggplant or 1 very small
      eggplant, diced**
  **2 medium tomatoes, peeled,
      seeded, and chopped**
  ¼ teaspoon basil
  ¼ teaspoon oregano
  2 tablespoons tomato purée
  1 teaspoon cornstarch
  1 tablespoon water
  Salt and pepper
  8 crepes
  Chopped parsley
  Tomato wedges
  Pitted black olives
  Grated Parmesan

Heat the oil and add the onion and garlic. Cook until soft and translucent. Add the green pepper, zucchini or cucumber, and eggplant. Cover and simmer over a gentle heat for 15 minutes. Add the tomatoes and the herbs and continue cooking uncovered for another 10 minutes.

Drain the vegetables and put into another bowl. To the pan juices, add tomato purée and 1 teaspoon cornstarch dissolved in 1 tablespoon water. Cook until thick. Adjust the seasoning, adding salt and pepper.

Place 2 tablespoons of the ratatouille in each crepe. Roll the crepes and place in a buttered oven-proof dish. Bake for 10 minutes in an oven preheated to 400°. Pour the sauce over the crepes. Garnish the dish with chopped parsley, tomato wedges and pitted black olives.

Ratatouille is an excellent vegetable dish on its own. Sprinkle with a little grated Parmesan and run under the broiler before serving.

vegetable crepes

Crepes can be wrapped around various vegetable combinations as attractive side dishes. The recipes listed here are just examples of possible side dishes and should not limit individual imaginations.

vegetable crepes

cauliflower crepes with mornay sauce

Yield: 8 servings
  1 small head cauliflower
  3 tablespoons butter
  3 tablespoons flour
  ½ cup light cream
  ½ cup milk
  ½ teaspoon salt
  8 crepes
  ½ cup dry bread crumbs
  1 tablespoon melted butter
  ¼ cup grated Parmesan cheese

Break cauliflower in small pieces and cook in salted water until soft. Drain. Melt butter; stir in flour and add cream, milk and salt. Cook over low heat until thickened, stirring continuously. Add cauliflower. Fill crepes; fold over and place in greased baking dish. Mix bread crumbs with butter and cheese. Sprinkle on tops of crepes. Bake at 350° for 15 minutes or until lightly browned.

creamed-mushroom crepes

Yield: 4 servings
  2 tablespoons butter
  2 tablespoons chopped green
      onions
  1 pound fresh mushrooms, sliced
  1 cup heavy cream
  ½ teaspoon salt
  ⅛ teaspoon pepper
  2 tablespoons flour
  2 tablespoons water
  ½ cup grated Gruyère cheese
  8 crepes
  Chopped parsley

Cook onions and mushrooms in hot butter until mushrooms are done. Add cream, salt, and pepper. Remove mushrooms with slotted spoon and reserve. Dissolve flour in water; stir into creamy mixture in pan. Simmer until thickened, stirring often. Add cheese and heat through. Fill crepes with mushrooms, roll up and place in greased baking pan. Spoon creamy sauce over crepes. Heat at 350° for 10 to 15 minutes. Garnish with parsley.

crepes with fresh mushrooms

Yield: 4 servings

½ pound fresh mushrooms
2 tablespoons butter
½ teaspoon salt
1 bouillon cube, crumbled
2 tablespoons sherry

¼ cup dairy sour cream
1 tablespoon minced chives
8 crepes
1 recipe tomato sauce

Slice mushrooms. Sauté in hot butter for several minutes. Add salt, bouillon cube and sherry. Cook until simmering. Stir in sour cream and chives. Heat until warm through. Spoon mixture onto center of crepes; fold and serve with tomato sauce spooned over the top.

crepes with fresh mushrooms

41

main-dish crepes

Crepe dishes can be the attractive center of a substantial meal or a light repast for the calorie-conscious diner. Portion sizes are easily controlled by the number of crepes eaten. Elementary mathematics helps regulate calorie intake better than in most dieting plans. Crepe dishes are also a convenient form of dining that can be eaten with the fingers or at a well-set table. Almost any main dish can be adapted for serving with crepes.

chicken-liver crepes in madeira sauce

Yield: 4 servings
**1 tablespoon butter plus 1
        tablespoon butter for sauce**
**4 green onions or 1 small onion,
        finely chopped**
2 pounds chicken livers
1 teaspoon paprika
2 tablespoons flour
**¼ cup chicken stock or chicken
        broth**
¼ cup heavy cream
2 tablespoons Madeira
8 crepes
Parsley for garnish

Heat the butter until foaming. Add the onion and cook until softened. Wash and cut chicken livers in half. Add the livers to the pan. Cook until lightly browned but still soft and tender. Remove the livers and onion from the pan.

In a clean saucepan melt the remaining 1 tablespoon butter and add paprika and flour. Add the juices from the chicken livers, the stock, cream and finally the Madeira. Cook over a moderate heat until thickened, stirring with a wire whisk.

Add 3 tablespoons of the sauce to the chicken livers and onions. Fill each crepe with 2 tablespoons of the chicken livers. Place in a buttered oven-proof pan and heat in a preheated oven at 400° for 15 minutes. Pour the rest of the sauce over the crepes just before serving. Sprinkle with finely chopped parsley.

cheese, bacon, and onion crepes

Yield: 6 servings
1 pound thinly sliced bacon
**10 green onions, with tops,
        chopped**
2 tablespoons butter
2 cups grated American cheese
12 crepes

Fry bacon until crisp. Drain and crumble. Pour off bacon fat from fry pan. Add butter, and heat. Stir in onions and cook for 3 minutes, until soft.

In each crepe, place a small amount of onions, and spoonfuls of bacon and cheese. Reserve enough cheese to sprinkle tops. Roll up each crepe and place in a buttered baking dish. Sprinkle tops with cheese. Bake at 400° for 15 minutes.

curried-lamb crepes

Yield: 6 servings

1½ pounds boneless lamb, cut
    into bite-size pieces
2 tablespoons butter
½ cup sliced onions
1 clove garlic, peeled
1½ cups milk
1 slice fresh ginger or ½ teaspoon
    ground ginger
2 teaspoons curry powder
½ teaspoon salt
½ teaspoon pepper
2 tablespoons lemon juice
Grated rind of 1 lemon
½ cup heavy cream
3 teaspoons cornstarch
1 tablespoon melted butter
2 ounces slivered almonds
12 crepes

Brown lamb in butter and add onions and whole clove of garlic. Sauté over low heat for 15 to 20 minutes. Remove garlic and add milk, ginger, curry powder, salt, pepper, lemon juice and grated lemon rind. Cook for 15 minutes. Mix cream with cornstarch. Add to curry mixture and stir until thickened.

Divide curry mixture between crepes; roll and place in a greased baking dish. Brush with melted butter and sprinkle with almonds. Bake at 400° for 12 minutes.

beef burgundy crepes

Yield: 4 to 6 servings

1 pound round or sirloin steak	½ teaspoon salt
2 strips bacon	⅛ teaspoon pepper
2 tablespoons butter	½ pound mushrooms, quartered
8 small white onions, peeled	2 tablespoons cornstarch
1 cup red wine	3 tablespoons cold water
1 cup beef bouillon	12 crepes
½ teaspoon thyme	

Cut the steak into bite-size pieces. Dice the bacon and fry in hot butter. When crisp, remove and set aside. Add onions and brown outsides. Set aside. Add meat and brown. Drain fat. Add wine, bouillon, bacon, onions, thyme and salt and pepper. Cover and simmer for 2 hours. Add the mushrooms. In a small bowl, add cornstarch to 3 tablespoons cold water. Mix well and stir into meat mixture. Cook until mixture thickens.

Put a spoonful or two in the center of each crepe. Roll and place seam side down in a baking dish. Spread remaining sauce over tops of crepes or brush with melted butter. Bake at 375° for 20 minutes.

beef and blue cheese crepes

Yield: 6 servings

1 pound ground beef (ground
    chuck or ground round)
½ cup chopped onions
2 tablespoons vegetable oil
½ cup finely chopped olives
½ cup blue cheese (or Roquefort)
1 cup dairy sour cream
1 egg, beaten
Salt and pepper to taste
12 crepes
2 tablespoons melted butter

Brown beef and onions in hot oil. Drain. Add olives. Crumble cheese and mix with sour cream and egg. Mix into beef mixture and cook over low heat for 5 minutes, stirring occasionally. Season to taste. Cool. Place 2 spoonfuls of the beef mixture along the center of each crepe; roll. Place in greased baking dish with seam side down. Brush tops of crepes with butter and bake at 375° for 20 minutes.

beef stroganoff crepes

Yield: 4 to 6 servings

1 pound boneless sirloin
1 tablespoon flour
½ teaspoon salt
2 tablespoons butter
¼ pound mushrooms, chopped
1 small onion, chopped
½ cup beef bouillon
1 cup dairy sour cream
1 tablespoon tomato paste or
    catsup
Sour cream for topping (optional)
12 crepes

Cut sirloin into ¼-inch strips. Combine flour and salt and coat meat. Heat butter and brown meat on both sides. Add mushrooms and onion and cook 3 or 4 minutes, until onion is tender. Add bouillon and cook for 3 minutes longer. Mix the tomato paste into the sour cream and stir into the meat mixture on low heat. Season to taste.

Divide mixture between crepes. Roll and turn seam side down in a greased baking dish. Top with more sour cream if desired and bake at 375° for 20 minutes.

crepes saint rafael

Yield: 4 servings

2 tablespoons butter
2 tablespoons flour
¼ teaspoon salt
1 cup milk
Dash of sherry
3 hard-cooked eggs, crumbled
5 ounces sweetbreads, parboiled
    and chopped

3 strips bacon, cooked and
    crumbled
1 tablespoon chopped chives
2 tablespoons grated cheese
1 tablespoon butter
8 warm crepes

Melt butter in saucepan over low heat. Blend in flour and salt. Mix well. Add milk all at once. Cook over moderate heat, stirring constantly, until mixture thickens and bubbles. Add sherry, crumbled eggs, sweetbreads, bacon and chives. Season to taste. Place a heaping tablespoon on each crepe, roll up and place in an oven-proof dish. Sprinkle with grated cheese, dot with butter, and bake in a preheated oven (400°) for 5 to 8 minutes or until the cheese has melted and crepes are hot throughout.

crepes with veal

Yield: 4 servings

**1 pound thin slices of veal, cut into
    1-inch squares
2 tablespoons flour
3 tablespoons vegetable oil
1 clove garlic, minced
2 tablespoons onions, chopped**

**1 tablespoon parsley
½ teaspoon basil
2 tomatoes, chopped
¼ cup heavy cream
Salt and pepper to taste
12 crepes**

Dredge veal with flour. Heat oil and fry the veal until lightly brown. Move meat to side of pan and sauté the minced garlic, onions, and parsley. Add the basil and tomatoes. Cook over medium heat until the tomatoes are soft. Break up with a fork and add cream, salt and pepper and cook over low heat until thoroughly heated. Cool.

Place a spoonful or two of filling in each crepe. Roll up and place seam side down in a greased baking dish. Bake at 350° for 30 minutes.

Other buffet dishes include: stuffed cabbage leaves, stuffed tomatoes, roast chicken, beet greens, quiche, cannelloni, fillet of veal, pork stuffing, and spinach.

crepes with veal

crepes à la bellman

Yield: 4 servings

bouillon

2 cubes chicken bouillon
2¼ cups water
1 teaspoon salt
2 to 3 white pepper corns
1 tablespoon onion, chopped
½ carrot, chopped

sauce

1 small veal sweetbread
3 ounces boiled ham
1 tablespoon onion
2 tablespoons butter
2½ tablespoons flour
¼ cup heavy cream
2 tablespoons grated cheese
8 warm crepes

Combine all ingredients for bouillon and bring to a simmer. Rinse sweetbread and boil in the bouillon for about 10 minutes. Skim, let cool in the bouillon. Remove the membranes around the sweetbread, chop the ham, onion and the sweetbread. Melt the butter, add the flour and brown lightly. Dilute with strained bouillon. Simmer the sauce for 3 to 4 minutes.

Add sweetbread, ham, onion and cream. Season to taste. Distribute the sauce on warm crepes; roll up. Place in greased baking dish. Sprinkle cheese on top and bake for 5 to 10 minutes at 425°.

ham and beef crepes

Yield: 4 servings

½ pound ground beef
1 cup chopped leftover ham
¼ cup flour
1 cup beef bouillon
¼ cup mushrooms, sliced
1 tablespoon butter
1 tablespoon flour

1 cup milk
3 tablespoons grated Swiss cheese
1 tablespoon grated Parmesan
   cheese
½ teaspoon prepared mustard
8 crepes

Cook ground beef over medium heat until slightly brown. Drain fat. Add ham and stir in ¼ cup flour. Add bouillon and sliced mushrooms. Bring to a simmer, stirring often. Cover and simmer for 30 minutes.

Meanwhile melt butter in a small saucepan. Remove from heat and add the flour, stirring with a wire whisk. Over a moderate heat, add the milk gradually, stirring the mixture constantly until the sauce is thickened. Add remaining ingredients, and salt and pepper to taste.

Fill crepes with meat mixture. Roll up and place in an oven-proof dish. Pour sauce over top. Bake at 375° for 25 minutes or until golden brown.

Step by step ham and beef crepes:

mix batter

cook in hot pan until bottom of crepe is browned

turn carefully with spatula and brown other side for a few seconds

assemble ingredients

fill crepes with meat mixture and roll up like a jelly roll

completed ham and beef crepes

crepes with swedish meatballs x

Yield: 6 servings

1 pound lean ground beef
1 cup soft bread crumbs
½ cup chopped onion
1 egg, slightly beaten
2 tablespoons chopped parsley
⅛ teaspoon ginger
⅛ teaspoon nutmeg
⅛ teaspoon pepper

1 tablespoon vegetable oil
2 tablespoons flour
1 bouillon cube, crumbled
½ cup milk
1 cup dairy sour cream
½ teaspoon salt
12 warm crepes

Combine beef with bread crumbs, onion, egg, parsley, ginger, nutmeg, and pepper. Form meatballs. Heat oil and add meatballs. Cook over moderate heat, turning several times, until done. Remove meatballs and keep warm. Stir flour and bouillon cube into meat juices. Add milk and stir over low heat until thickened. Mix in sour cream and salt and heat but do not boil. Divide meatballs between crepes and fold over. Spoon sauce over filled crepes and serve.

crepes with hamburger stroganoff x

Yield: 6 servings

1 small onion, chopped
1 tablespoon vegetable oil
1 pound lean ground beef
1 can cream of mushroom soup,
    undiluted
½ teaspoon salt
2 tablespoons catsup
1 4-ounce can mushrooms,
    drained
½ cup sour cream
12 crepes
2 tablespoons melted butter

Sauté onion in oil, add ground beef, and cook until browned. Pour off fat. Mix in soup, salt, catsup and mushrooms. Heat to boiling. Remove from heat and stir in sour cream. Fill crepes with mixture and fold over. Place in shallow baking pan. Brush with butter. Heat in 350° oven for 15 minutes.

ⅹ cheese layer crepes

Yield: 4 servings
   1 medium onion, chopped
   ⅓ cup vegetable oil
   1 pound ground beef
   ¼ cup flour
   8-ounce can tomato sauce
   1 bouillon cube dissolved in 1 cup
       boiling water
   1 bay leaf
   1 teaspoon salt
   ⅛ teaspoon pepper
   1 package cheese sauce mix
   Milk for cheese sauce
   ¾ cup cheddar cheese, grated
   2 tablespoons Parmesan cheese
   6 crepes

Heat vegetable oil and fry onion gently for 5 minutes or until tender. Add meat and cook for 5 minutes. Drain off fat. Stir in flour and remove pan from heat. Add tomato sauce and thoroughly blend. Add bouillon, bay leaf, and seasonings. Cover and simmer gently for 40 minutes.

Make up cheese sauce mix according to package directions. Place 1 crepe in bottom of baking dish; spread a layer of meat, then a layer of sauce. Sprinkle with cheddar cheese. Continue these layers, ending with a layer of sauce. Sprinkle Parmesan on top. Bake in a 350° oven for 30 minutes or until golden brown.

cheese layer crepes

crepes with welsh rarebit sauce

Yield: 4 servings

1 tablespoon cornstarch
2 cups grated sharp cheddar cheese
¾ cup milk
1 teaspoon dry mustard
1 egg, well-beaten

8 crepes
¼ cup bacon bits or 8 strips bacon,
    cooked and crumbled
1 tomato, chopped

In mixing bowl combine cornstarch and cheese. Add milk and mustard. Heat until cheese melts. Stir often. Add a small amount of hot mixture to egg; return to hot mixture. Cook and stir over low heat until mixture thickens and is creamy. In shallow baking pan, fill crepes with bacon bits and half of the rarebit sauce; fold crepes over. Pour remaining sauce over all and top with tomatoes. Broil until sauce is bubbly.

hot dogs in crepes

Yield: 5 or 6 servings

6 long hot dogs
Saurkraut
Swiss cheese, grated

Cook the hot dogs and saurkraut together and roll each hot dog with some saurkraut into a crepe. Top the rolled crepes with the grated Swiss cheese and place in an oven-proof dish. Heat at 425° until the cheese browns. Serve hot.

hot dogs in crepes

crepes with cottage cheese

crepes with cottage cheese

Yield: 4 to 6 servings

8 ounces cottage cheese

Batter for 12 crepes

Mix ¼ cup cottage cheese into batter before frying crepes. As crepes are cooked, lay in a lightly greased oven-proof dish and sprinkle each layer with cottage cheese. Bake at 325° for 10 minutes. Serve the warm crepes with a tossed salad.

spinach and ham crepes

Yield: 4 servings
  1 pound spinach
  1 cup boiled ham, finely chopped
  3 tablespoons heavy cream
  Pinch of salt
  Pinch of nutmeg
  (1 tablespoon cornstarch)
  (2 tablespoons cold water)
  2 tablespoons butter
  8 crepes
  Pieces of ham or bacon for garnish

Discard the stems and heavy veins of the spinach and wash it to remove grains of sand. Cook spinach about 5 minutes in plenty of boiling water. Drain the spinach.

Chop the ham finely and place half of it in the blender. Add the spinach, cream, salt and nutmeg. Turn on the motor. You may need to add a little more cream if the blades of the blender become jammed. Return the mixture to a clean saucepan and add the remainder of the chopped ham. Stir over a low heat. If the purée appears too thin, add 1 tablespoon cornstarch dissolved in 2 tablespoons cold water and it will thicken immediately. Spread the ham and spinach purée on a crepe. Fold the crepe into a triangle and place in a buttered oven-proof dish. Dot the crepes with butter. Heat for 15 minutes in a preheated 400° oven. Garnish with pieces of ham or bacon. May be served with a Mornay or Hollandaise sauce.

spinach and ham crepes

ham and asparagus crepes

Yield: 6 servings
12 thin slices boiled ham
1 pound asparagus
Mornay or Hollandaise sauce
12 crepes
2 tablespoons butter

Peel the lower third of each asparagus spear and simmer, uncovered, in plenty of lightly salted water for about 15 minutes or until tender.

Spread out the crepes and cover each crepe with a slice of ham. Over the ham place 2 or 3 asparagus spears and roll up the crepes. Place the crepes in a buttered oven-proof dish. Dot the surface of the crepes with butter and bake in a preheated 400° oven for 15 minutes. Cover with Mornay or Hollandaise sauce.

mushroom crepes with ham

Yield: 4 servings
3 tablespoons butter
3 green onions or ½ onion, finely chopped
1½ cups mushrooms, thinly sliced
2 tablespoons lemon juice
½ cup chicken broth
8 thin slices of boiled ham
½ cup grated Swiss or Gruyère cheese
¼ cup heavy cream
Salt and pepper
1 tablespoon cornstarch dissolved in 2 tablespoons cold water
8 crepes
2 tablespoons butter

Sauté the onion in the butter until soft. Add the mushrooms. Sprinkle the mushrooms with lemon juice to prevent discoloration. Cook the mushrooms for 1 minute. Add the chicken broth and cook over a high heat, uncovered, for 1 more minute. Lower the heat and add the grated cheese and cream. Do not heat the cheese too quickly or it will spin into threads. Add the cornstarch dissolved in water and the mixture will thicken immediately. It should be thick enough to hold its shape in the rolled crepe. Adjust the seasoning, adding salt and pepper to taste.

Lay a piece of boiled ham on each crepe. Put about 3 tablespoons of the mushroom mixture over the ham and roll the crepes. Place in a buttered oven-proof dish and dot the crepes with butter. Bake in a preheated 400° oven for 15 minutes and serve immediately.

ham-filled crepes

Yield: 4 servings
  **2 cups cooked ham, finely
    chopped**
  **2 hard-cooked eggs, finely
    chopped**
  ¼ cup chopped ripe olives
  2 teaspoons sweet pickle relish
  ¾ cup mayonnaise
  8 crepes
  8 slices Swiss cheese

Combine ham, eggs, olives, relish, and mayonnaise. Divide mixture between crepes and roll up. Place in shallow baking pan with 1 slice of cheese on each filled crepe. Broil until cheese melts.

mushroom-ham crepes

Yield: 6 servings
  ½ pound mushrooms, chopped
  4 tablespoons butter
  2 cups leftover ham
  2 tablespoons Madeira wine
  2 tablespoons flour
  1 cup beef bouillon
  Salt and pepper to taste
  12 crepes

Fry mushrooms in hot butter for 1 minute and add ham. Continue cooking for 2 minutes. Add Madeira wine and flour mixed with a small amount of cold bouillon. Stir in rest of bouillon and cook for 10 minutes, stirring occasionally, until sauce is thickened. Season to taste.

Place 1 or 2 spoonfuls in each crepe. Roll, and place in a greased baking dish. Spread any leftover sauce over the tops of the crepes. Bake at 375° for 20 minutes.

easy turkey-spinach crepes

Yield: 4 servings
- 1 cup diced cooked turkey (or chicken)
- ½ cup cooked chopped spinach, drained
- ¼ cup dry bread crumbs
- ⅓ cup grated Parmesan cheese
- 1 tablespoon minced onion
- 1 can cream of chicken soup (undiluted)
- 8 crepes
- ½ cup milk
- ¼ cup slivered almonds

Mix turkey, spinach, bread crumbs, cheese, onion, and ½ can condensed soup. Fill crepes and roll up. Place in shallow baking dish. Combine rest of soup with milk and pour over crepes. Sprinkle with almonds. Heat at 350° for 15 minutes.

crepes with cashew-chicken filling

Yield: 6 servings
- 3 tablespoons butter
- ½ cup cashew nuts, coarsely chopped
- 2 cups uncooked chicken, chopped
- 1 cup thinly sliced broccoli
- 1 onion, sliced
- 1½ cups chicken bouillon
- 2 tablespoons cornstarch
- 2 tablespoons soy sauce
- 12 warm crepes

Heat butter and cook cashews until lightly toasted. Remove nuts from pan. In remaining butter, stir in chicken and broccoli; cook about 5 minutes, turning mixture often. Add onions and bouillon. Cover and cook for 6 to 8 minutes. Dissolve cornstarch in soy sauce; stir into chicken mixture. Stir over medium heat until thickened. Add cashews. Fill crepes and serve immediately.

chicken crepe soufflé

Yield: 6 servings
  5 cups chicken, minced
  1 pound mushrooms, chopped
  1 lemon, juiced
  2 egg yolks
  ½ cup cream

bechamel sauce

  2 tablespoons butter   **½ teaspoon salt**
  ¼ cup flour   **⅛ teaspoon white pepper**
  2 cups cold milk

To make sauce, melt butter and blend in flour. Cook for 3 minutes, stirring constantly. Add the milk, salt and pepper and cook until thickened. Add the chicken, mushrooms, lemon juice, egg yolks and cream to the sauce. Mix well.

Butter a round soufflé mold or an oven-proof bowl and place crepes on the bottom and sides. Fill with chicken mixture and place crepes on top. Bake in a moderate oven (350°) for 30 minutes. Unmold on a warm platter and serve with extra Bechamel Sauce. It is delicious and unusual.

chicken crepe soufflé

chicken in white wine crepes

Yield: 6 servings

3 tablespoons butter
3 tablespoons minced green
    onions
3 cups chicken, diced
1 cup cooked ham, diced
½ teaspoon salt
⅛ teaspoon pepper
½ teaspoon tarragon
½ cup dry white wine
½ cup canned mushrooms
1 hard-cooked egg, diced
A double recipe Veloute sauce
12 crepes
2 tablespoons melted butter

Sauté onions in hot butter for 1 minute. Stir in chicken, ham, salt, pepper and tarragon. Stir mixture on high heat for 2 minutes. Pour in wine and boil down until the liquid has almost disappeared. Mix in mushrooms and egg. Fold in Veloute sauce. Divide mixture between crepes and roll up. Place in a greased baking dish and brush tops with melted butter. Heat at 350° for 10 minutes.

quick chicken divan crepes

Yield: 6 servings

1 10-ounce package frozen
    chopped broccoli
1 can cream of chicken soup
    (undiluted)
½ teaspoon Worcestershire sauce
¾ cup grated Parmesan cheese
2 cups cooked chicken, cut into
    small strips
12 crepes
⅓ cup mayonnaise
1 tablespoon milk

Cook broccoli according to package directions; drain. Combine with soup, Worcestershire sauce, ½ cup of the cheese, and chicken. Divide mixture between crepes, roll up, and place in a shallow baking dish. Combine mayonnaise with milk; spread over crepes. Sprinkle with ¼ cup cheese and broil until cheese bubbles.

chicken-filled crepes x

Yield: 4 servings

white sauce

3 tablespoons butter
¼ cup flour
¼ teaspoon salt
1 cup milk

filling

1 tablespoon sherry or 1 teaspoon
    lemon juice
1½ cups finely diced cooked
    chicken
¼ cup finely chopped almonds
1 tablespoon finely minced onion

⅓ cup mayonnaise
1 egg white stiffly beaten
2 tablespoons grated Parmesan
    cheese
8 crepes

Prepare white sauce by melting butter and blending in flour and salt. Add milk all at once. Cook quickly, stirring constantly, until the mixture thickens and bubbles.

Combine white sauce, sherry, chicken, almonds and onion. Divide the mixture between the crepes, spreading it on each one. Roll up and place 2 rolls in individual serving dishes. Fold mayonnaise into the egg white and spread over crepes. Sprinkle with cheese. Bake at 375° for 10 minutes.

crepes with hot chicken salad x

Yield: 6 servings

2 cups diced cooked chicken
2 cups celery, chopped
3 tablespoons onion, minced
½ teaspoon salt
½ teaspoon pepper
½ cup pecans, chopped

¾ cup mayonnaise
1 small can sliced mushrooms,
    drained
1 can cream of chicken soup
12 warm crepes

Mix all filling ingredients. Divide between crepes and roll up. Place in large greased oven-proof baking dish or in 6 individual baking dishes. Cook at 300° for 30 minutes.

oriental beef and pepper crepes

Yield: 6 servings

1½ pounds sirloin steak, sliced into ⅛-inch slivers
2 green peppers, sliced into rings
3 tablespoons vegetable oil
3 cups thinly sliced onions
¾ teaspoon salt
1 clove garlic, crushed
3 green onions, thinly sliced

1½ teaspoons sugar
⅓ cup sherry
½ teaspoon ginger
¾ cup beef bouillon
3 tablespoons cornstarch
¾ cup water
2 tablespoons soy sauce
12 crepes

Heat oil in fry pan. Add green pepper rings, onion slices, salt, garlic, and green onions. Cook, stirring over high heat, for 3 minutes. Add beef slivers and cook, stirring over high heat, for 2 minutes. Stir in sugar, sherry, and ginger. Cook for 1 minute. Add bouillon and bring mixture to a boil.

In a small bowl, combine cornstarch, water and soy sauce. Stir into beef mixture and cook until sauce is thickened.

Divide mixture between warm crepes, roll up and serve. Pour any remaining juices over tops.

hawaiian crepes

Yield: 6 servings

2 tablespoons butter
1 medium onion, sliced
1 green pepper, cut into small strips
1 8-ounce can pineapple chunks with syrup
1 tablespoon honey
1 tablespoon vinegar

1 tablespoon soy sauce
2 tablespoons cornstarch
1 cup chicken bouillon
2 cups cooked chicken, cut in small pieces
¼ cup cashews, chopped
12 crepes

Melt butter and cook onion and green pepper until soft. Add pineapple, honey, vinegar and soy sauce. Dissolve cornstarch in bouillon and add to pineapple mixture. Cook, stirring, until thickened. Stir in chicken and cashews. Heat. Fill warm crepes and fold. Serve immediately.

chinese spring rolls fried in oil

Yield: 4 servings

Batter for 16 crepes
Vegetable oil for deep-fat frying
1 can bean sprouts
6 ounces pork, minced (about ¾ cup)
1 large onion, minced

1 can bamboo shoots, sliced thin
1½ tablespoons soy sauce
1 teaspoon freshly ground black pepper
1 egg white or 2 tablespoons flour and ¼ cup water

Rinse bean sprouts in cold water; drain well. Heat 1½ tablespoons vegetable oil in pan and fry pork and onion for about 4 minutes. Add bean sprouts, bamboo shoots, soy sauce and pepper. Fry for 2 minutes while stirring.

Make crepes, frying on one side only. Distribute the filling on the fried side of the crepes. Fold in sides and roll up like small parcels. Seal with egg white or with flour stirred in a small amount of water. Deep fat fry in oil at 400° until golden brown. Drain on paper towels. Serve immediately with soy sauce and a large green salad.

chinese spring rolls fried in oil

shrimp and water chestnut crepes

Yield: 6 servings

2 scallions, thinly sliced
2 tablespoons butter
1 pound shrimp, cooked and
    peeled
¼ pound mushrooms, finely
    chopped
1 can water chestnuts, chopped

3 tablespoons butter
3 tablespoons flour
¼ teaspoon salt
1 cup milk
¼ cup heavy cream
1 lemon, sliced
12 warm crepes

Sauté scallions in butter for 2 minutes. Reserve several shrimp for garnish. Slice the rest of the shrimp into ⅓-inch slices. Add shrimp and mushrooms to scallions and cook 2 minutes. Add water chestnuts and remove from heat while preparing the cream sauce.

Melt butter in saucepan over low heat. Blend in flour and salt. Mix well. Add milk all at once. Cook over moderate heat, stirring constantly, until mixture thickens and bubbles. Add cream a little at a time, blending thoroughly. Stir into shrimp mixture.

Fill crepes and roll. Turn seam side down in a buttered baking dish. Bake 10 to 15 minutes in a 375° oven. Garnish with reserved shrimp and lemon slices. Can be served with pork chops and orange sauce.

imitation chinese egg rolls

Yield: 6 servings

1 cup chopped cooked pork
1 16-ounce can Chinese
    vegetables, drained
¼ cup minced green onions
½ teaspoon ground ginger
2 teaspoons soy sauce
1 teaspoon sugar
12 warm cooked crepes
Hot oil for deep-fat frying

Mix pork with Chinese vegetables, onions, ginger, soy sauce, and sugar. Place about 2 tablespoons mixture on each crepe, fold over sides, and roll up. Seal edges with leftover crepe batter or a little flour-water mixture. Cook in hot oil at 375° until golden brown. Drain. Serve hot.

Picture on next page: shrimp and water chestnut crepes served with pork chops and orange sauce

sweet-and-sour-pork crepes

Yield: 6 servings
  1 tablespoon soy sauce
  2 tablespoons sherry
  ¼ cup cornstarch
  1½ pounds lean pork, cut into
      ½-inch cubes
  Vegetable oil for deep-fat frying
  ½ cup sugar
  1 tablespoon catsup
  ¼ cup vinegar
  ½ cup pineapple juice (from can of
      chunks)
  1 tablespoon cornstarch
  2 tablespoons water
  2 tablespoons vegetable oil
  1 green pepper, cut in ½-inch
      slices
  1 medium carrot, cut in ½-inch
      slices
  1 clove garlic, minced
  1 cup pineapple chunks
  12 crepes

Mix soy sauce, sherry, and cornstarch and coat pork cubes. Heat enough vegetable oil to cover pork cubes. When oil is very hot, carefully add half the cubes of pork. Cook 5 to 7 minutes and turn frequently. Remove from pan and cook the remaining cubes.

Combine sugar, catsup, vinegar and pineapple juice. Mix cornstarch with 2 tablespoons of water before combining with pineapple mixture. Cook until sauce comes to a boil and becomes thick and clear.

Heat the 2 tablespoons oil in a frying pan and add green pepper, carrot, and garlic. Stir and fry over high heat. Add pineapple chunks, pork and sauce. Cook for 5 minutes.

Place 2 spoonfuls in the center of each crepe. Roll up and place seam side down in a buttered baking dish. Brush tops with remaining sauce and bake at 375° for about 20 minutes.

creamed-oyster crepes

Yield: 4 servings
  1 pint oysters
  2 tablespoons butter
  2 tablespoons flour
  1 cup oyster liquor (add cream to
      make 1 cup)
  ½ teaspoon salt
  ½ teaspoon curry powder
  1 teaspoon lemon juice
  8 warm crepes
  Chopped parsley for garnish

Drain oysters and pat dry with paper towels. Save the liquor. Melt butter and blend in flour. Stir in oyster liquor slowly. Add salt and curry powder. Heat to simmer temperature and add oysters. Heat oysters thoroughly but do not boil. Season with lemon juice. Divide between warm crepes and roll up. Add parsley garnish.

crepes romaine

Yield: 4 servings
  1 tablespoon onion, chopped
  1 tablespoon butter
  1 tablespoon flour
  1 cup light cream
  4 ounces smoked salmon, diced
  3 hard-cooked eggs, chopped
  1 to 2 tablespoons capers
  ½ teaspoon chopped dill
  ½ teaspoon fresh lemon juice
  2 tablespoons grated cheese
  1 tablespoon butter
  8 warm crepes

Fry onion in butter until soft. Stir in flour. Add cream a little at a time. Let simmer for 3 to 4 minutes and then add rest of ingredients. Season to taste. Place a heaping tablespoon on each crepe, roll up and place in a buttered oven-proof dish. Sprinkle with grated cheese, dot with butter, and bake in a preheated oven (400°) for 5 to 8 minutes or until the cheese has melted and crepes are hot throughout.

Picture on next page: crepes romaine

shrimp crepes with veloute sauce

Yield: 8 servings
**1 pound small shrimp, cooked,
    peeled and deveined
4 egg whites
½ cup heavy cream
½ teaspoon salt
¼ teaspoon pepper
16 crepes
Double recipe Veloute sauce**

Chop half the shrimp into 4 or 5 pieces each. Beat egg whites until stiff. Beat cream until stiff. Combine cream and egg whites; add seasonings and chopped shrimp. Divide mixture between crepes. Roll and turn seam side down in a buttered baking dish. Pour sauce over the tops of the crepes. Bake at 350° for 20 minutes. During last three minutes, add rest of shrimp for garnish and heat only to warm.

crab crepes with tomatoes and herbs

Yield: 4 servings
**12-ounce can or ¾ pound fresh
    crab meat
2 medium tomatoes, skinned and
    seeds removed
1 green pepper, diced
3 green onions
Mornay sauce**

**Juice of 1 lemon
1 tablespoon butter
¼ cup heavy cream
1 tablespoon chives combined
    with parsley, finely chopped
8 crepes**

Clean the crab and set aside. Remove the skin and seeds from the tomatoes. Melt the butter and sauté the green onions and green pepper over a moderate heat for about 4 minutes.

Prepare a Mornay sauce.

In a bowl, combine the crab meat, tomatoes, and green pepper-onion mixture. Add the lemon juice, cream, and herbs. Add about ½ of the prepared sauce. Place 2 tablespoons of the mixture in each crepe. Place the crepes in a buttered oven-proof dish and spoon the remainder of the sauce over the crepes. Heat in a preheated oven at 400° for 15 minutes, until the sauce is golden brown and bubbling. Sprinkle with chives and parsley.

Picture on next page: shrimp crepes with veloute sauce

creamed-crab in crepes

Yield: 6 servings

2 tablespoons butter
3 tablespoons minced green onions
1½ cups crab meat, shredded
½ teaspoon salt
⅛ teaspoon pepper
¼ cup dry white wine

2 tablespoons cornstarch
2 tablespoons milk
1½ cups heavy cream
½ cup grated Swiss cheese
12 crepes
¼ cup grated Swiss cheese
2 tablespoons butter

Heat butter and stir in onions and crab meat. Stir over high heat for 1 minute. Season and add white wine. Boil mixture until wine has almost evaporated. Remove mixture and reserve.

Blend cornstarch with milk and add to skillet with cream. Simmer for 2 minutes and blend in cheese. Stir continuously until cheese is melted. Blend half the sauce with crab mixture.

Divide mixture between crepes and roll up. Place in a buttered baking dish and spoon rest of sauce over tops of crepes. Sprinkle with cheese and dot with butter. Bake at 425° for 6 to 8 minutes or until cheese is lightly browned.

crab-filled crepewich

Yield: 4 servings

4 ounces fresh, frozen, or canned crab meat
¼ cup thinly sliced green onions
1 tablespoon lemon juice
1 tablespoon chili sauce
4 crepes
¼ cup mayonnaise
2 egg yolks, beaten
¼ cup grated Swiss cheese
2 egg whites

Drain and flake crab meat. Mix crab, onions, lemon juice, and chili sauce. Spread on crepes. Combine mayonnaise with yolks and cheese. Beat egg whites to form stiff peaks and fold into mayonnaise mixture. Spread over layer of crab filling on crepes. Place open face under broiler and broil until brown.

manicotti

Yield: 6 to 8 servings

3 eggs
½ teaspoon salt
2 pounds ricotta cheese
¾ cup Parmesan or Romano
   cheese

¼ teaspoon pepper
½ pound Mozzarella, cut into 12
   strips
12 to 14 crepes
3 cans (8 ounces each) tomato sauce

Mix eggs, salt, ricotta, ¼ cup Parmesan, and pepper. Place about 2 tablespoons of filling and a strip of Mozzarella on each crepe and roll up.

Pour 1 can tomato sauce into a large baking dish. Place crepes, seam side down in sauce and sprinkle with ½ cup Parmesan cheese. Cover crepes with remaining 2 cans of sauce. Bake in preheated 350° oven for 45 minutes.

crepes with spaghetti sauce

Yield: 4 to 5 servings

Prepare 2 cups of a favorite recipe of spaghetti sauce. Add meat, sausage, or mushrooms. If sauce is runny, add enough tomato paste to thicken. Fill 8 to 10 crepes, roll and place in baking dish. Spread extra sauce over the tops of crepes and sprinkle with grated Parmesan cheese. Bake at 400° for 15 minutes.

pizza crepes

Yield: 6 servings

6 crepes
1 tablespoon vegetable oil
½ cup tomato sauce
½ teaspoon oregano
¼ teaspoon basil
¼ cup pepperoni, cut into thin
   slices
¼ cup sliced mushrooms
¾ cup grated Mozzarella cheese
¼ cup grated Parmesan cheese

Brush crepes with oil and spread with tomato sauce. Sprinkle with herbs and top with pepperoni, mushrooms and cheese. Broil open-face until bubbly.

cannelloni crepes

Yield: 4 servings

1 medium onion, finely chopped
2 tablespoons vegetable oil
¾ pound ground beef
2 tablespoons tomato sauce
½ cup flour
1 beef bouillon cube dissolved in 1
    cup boiling water
⅓ cup mushrooms, sliced

½ teaspoon salt
⅛ teaspoon pepper
2 tablespoons butter
1¼ cups milk
⅓ cup cheddar or Parmesan
    cheese, grated
8 warm crepes
Watercress

Fry onions in hot vegetable oil for 5 minutes. Add meat and cook for 5 minutes. Remove from heat and stir in tomato sauce and ¼ cup flour. Add bouillon, sliced mushrooms, and seasonings. Cover and simmer for 45 minutes. Meanwhile, melt butter in a separate small pan. Stir in ¼ cup flour and cook for 2 minutes. Remove from heat and gradually stir in 1¼ cups milk. Bring to a boil while stirring. Blend in ¼ cup cheese. Remove from heat; leave cover on.

Fill warm crepes with ground beef mixture and roll up. Place them in a baking dish and pour the sauce over them. Sprinkle with remaining cheese and broil for about 3 minutes or until golden. Serve at once. (Garnish with watercress.)

italian meat crepes

Yield: 6 servings
1 pound ground beef
6 ounces Italian sausage
¾ teaspoon Italian seasoning
4 ounces shredded mozzarella
3 cups spaghetti sauce
12 to 14 crepes
Parmesan cheese for topping

Brown meat and sausage. Add seasoning, cheese, and 1 cup spaghetti sauce. Fill crepe with 2 to 3 tablespoons of meat mixture. Roll up, and place seam side down in shallow baking dish with a thin layer of sauce. Pour and cover crepes with sauce and sprinkle with Parmesan cheese. Bake in moderate oven until bubbly—about 25 minutes.

cannelloni crepes

beef and bean sprout crepes

Yield: 8 servings

1½ pounds flank steak
1 16-ounce can bean sprouts
¼ cup butter
1 green pepper, cut in 1-inch strips

1 cup beef bouillon
2 tablespoons soy sauce
16 crepes

Slice steak in paper thin strips and then into bite-size pieces. Drain bean sprouts. Brown meat in hot butter. Add the bean sprouts, green pepper, bouillon and soy sauce. Cook together for 2 to 3 minutes, until steak is just done.

Fill crepes with mixture and roll up. Place seam side down in a greased baking dish. Pour extra pan liquid over crepes. Bake at 375° for 20 minutes.

china crepes

Yield: 4 servings

8 warm crepes
2 pork chops or 9 ounces pork
    shoulder or ham
½ teaspoon curry
½ teaspoon paprika
1 green pepper, cubed
2 green onions, minced
8 ounces shrimp, peeled and
    deveined
1 can bean sprouts
1 red pepper, cubed
1 to 2 teaspoons soy sauce
1 to 2 tablespoons sherry or white
    wine, if desired
2 tablespoons grated cheese, if
    desired
2 tablespoons butter

Cut the meat into thin strips and brown. Sprinkle with curry and paprika. Add the green onions and peppers and continue to fry for 5 to 10 minutes. Add the heated bean sprouts and shrimp. Season with soy sauce and wine if desired.

Spread the filling on the crepes, roll up and place seam down on a greased baking dish. Sprinkle with grated cheese if desired and a few pats of butter. Bake in oven at 400° for 10 to 15 minutes.

china crepes

flaming shellfish crepes

Yield: 4 servings

4 tablespoons butter
3 drops Tabasco sauce
1/8 teaspoon salt
Dash pepper
2 cups milk
2 egg yolks
3 tablespoons sherry

1/2 pound cooked crab meat
1 pound cooked, deveined shrimp
1 small can mushroom pieces,
    drained
8 crepes
Brandy

Make white sauce by adding butter, Tabasco sauce, and seasonings to milk. Add beaten egg yolks and cook over low heat until thickened. Blend in remaining ingredients except brandy. Place crepes in single-serving baking dishes. Fill cavity with shrimp-crab mixture. Bake at 350° for 5 to 10 minutes. Sprinkle with warmed brandy and ignite. Serve immediately.

beef and snow peas crepes

Yield: 6 servings

1 pound flank steak, sliced as thin
    as possible
1/4 cup soy sauce
2 tablespoons sherry
2 teaspoons cornstarch
2 green onions, thinly sliced
3 tablespoons vegetable oil
1 package frozen snow peas (pea
    pods), defrosted
1/2 cup chicken bouillon
12 crepes

Marinate steak in a mixture of soy sauce, sherry, cornstarch, and onions for 30 minutes. Brown the meat quickly in 2 tablespoons of hot vegetable oil over high heat. Stir continuously. Remove from pan. Add rest of vegetable oil. When hot, stir in snow peas and cook until pods are beginning to soften. Return steak to pan and add chicken bouillon. Cook for 2 to 3 minutes.

Fill warm crepes and serve immediately.

baked chinese spring rolls with cabbage

Yield: 4 to 6 servings

9 ounces white cabbage
2 tablespoons vegetable oil
1 tablespoon soy sauce
1 teaspoon salt
¼ teaspoon pepper

9 ounces pork, minced (about 1 cup)
1 green onion, minced
Batter for 12 to 16 crepes

Slice the cabbage into fine strips and fry in oil until partially soft. Add the soy sauce, salt, and pepper, and cook 2 minutes more. In a separate pan fry the pork with the green onion until done. Mix with cabbage.

Fry crepes on one side only. When done, place filling on browned side of crepes. Wrap up like a parcel. Place crepes in a lightly greased oven-proof dish and brush with soy and oil. Bake in oven at 400° for about 15 minutes.

baked chinese spring rolls with cabbage

chicken and oyster crepes

Yield: 6 servings
  1 pint oysters
  1 cup milk
  1 teaspoon butter
  ¼ teaspoon oregano
  **2 cups cooked chicken cut into
      small pieces**
  ½ cup cooked diced potatoes
  1 tablespoon butter
  1 tablespoon flour
  Salt
  Dash of cayenne pepper
  1 egg yolk
  1 teaspoon heavy cream
  **Finely chopped parsley for
      garnish**
  12 crepes

Put the oysters with their liquor into a small saucepan with ½ cup milk and 1 teaspoon butter.

Add ¼ teaspoon oregano. After the milk has reached simmering point, continue to cook at a gentle simmer for 6 minutes.

Drain the oysters and put in a bowl with the shredded chicken and diced potatoes.

Melt 1 tablespoon butter and when foaming remove from the heat and add 1 tablespoon flour. Gradually add the liquor in which the oysters were cooked. Continue to cook over a gentle heat until the sauce has thickened. Check the seasoning and add salt and a dash of cayenne pepper to taste.

Enrich the sauce by combining 1 egg yolk with 1 teaspoon cream. Add 2 tablespoons of the hot sauce to the egg yolk and cream and return to the sauce in the saucepan. This will improve the color and the taste of the sauce. Add 3 tablespoons of the thick sauce to the chicken, oysters and potatoes. Put 2 tablespoons of the mixture into each crepe. Roll the crepes and place in a buttered oven-proof dish to cook at 400° for 15 minutes. Pour the remaining sauce over the crepes. Sprinkle some finely chopped parsley over the sauce just before serving.

crispy tuna-noodle crepes

Yield: 4 servings
⅓ cup chopped onion
⅓ cup chopped green pepper
2 tablespoons butter
⅓ cup mayonnaise
1 tablespoon prepared mustard
¼ cup milk
1 7-ounce can tuna
¼ teaspoon salt
¼ teaspoon pepper
1 can Chinese noodles
12 warm crepes

Cook onion and green pepper in hot butter until tender. Mix mayonnaise, mustard, and milk; stir until smooth. Add tuna, salt, pepper, onion and green pepper to mayonnaise mixture. Just before serving, fold in the Chinese noodles; fill warm crepes, and roll. Serve immediately.

tuna fish or salmon crepes

Yield: 6 servings
1½ cups tuna or salmon
1 tablespoon capers
1 tablespoon finely chopped
    gherkins
1 hard-boiled egg, chopped
1 tablespoon parsley, finely
    chopped
1 tablespoon enriched Bechamel
    sauce or Russian dressing
6 crepes

Combine the above filling ingredients and put 2 tablespoons in each crepe. Roll the crepes and place in a buttered oven-proof dish. Place in a preheated 400° oven for 15 minutes. Cover with an enriched Bechamel sauce or Russian dressing.

tuna with herbs crepes

Yield: 4 servings
  1 6½-ounce can tuna, drained
  3 hard-cooked eggs, peeled and
      chopped
  ½ cup mayonnaise
  1 teaspoon prepared mustard
  ¼ teaspoon salt
  ⅛ teaspoon pepper
  1 tablespoon sweet pickle relish
  1 tablespoon chopped parsley
  ½ teaspoon dried tarragon
  ½ teaspoon dried chervil
  8 crepes
  2 tablespoons melted butter

Break tuna into small chunks. Combine tuna, eggs, mayonnaise, mustard, salt, pepper, relish, parsley, tarragon, and chervil. Divide mixture between crepes and roll up. Brush tops with butter. Heat at 350° for 20 minutes or until crepes are hot throughout.

down-east lobster crepes

Yield: 4 servings
  ¼ cup butter
  2 tablespoons flour
  1½ cups light cream
  3 egg yolks, beaten
  ½ pound cooked lobster, chunked
  ¼ teaspoon paprika
  ¼ teaspoon salt
  ⅛ teaspoon pepper
  ¼ cup dry white wine
  8 crepes
  Parsley to garnish

Melt butter and blend in flour. Add cream and cook over low heat, stirring constantly, until thickened. Stir 2 tablespoons hot mixture into egg yolks; then place egg yolks in pan. Cook over low heat, stirring constantly, until thickend. Add lobster, paprika, salt, pepper, and wine. Place crepes in shallow baking pan. Fill crepes with lobster mixture and fold over. Pour remaining sauce over crepes. Heat in 350° oven for 15 minutes or until hot. Garnish with parsley.

lobster crepes
(fruit of the sea crepes)

Yield: 4 servings
   1 4½-pound lobster or 2 cups of
      cooked shrimp, flounder, and
      scallops in any proportion
   1 tablespoon tomato paste
   Mornay sauce
   2 tablespoons butter
   8 crepes

Poach the fish in salted water held at simmering point. The lobster will cook in 20 minutes. Other seafoods will cook in 8 to 10 minutes.

Cut the fish into small pieces and place in a bowl with the tomato paste.

Prepare a Mornay sauce.

Combine half of the sauce with the lobster or combination of seafoods.

Place about 2 to 3 tablespoons of the seafood in each crepe. Roll the crepes. Place the crepes in a buttered oven-proof dish. Dot the surface of the crepes with butter and bake in a preheated 400° oven for 15 minutes. Serve with the remainder of the sauce. Garnish the dish with lobster tails or shrimp, parsley, and lemon wedges.

smoked salmon and cream cheese crepes

Yield: 6 servings
   8 ounces cream cheese
   3 tablespoons cold Bechamel
      (white) sauce
   ½ pound smoked salmon
   1 tablespoon butter
   6 crepes
   Parsley sprigs

Soften the cream cheese with the cold white sauce and spread 2 tablespoons of the cheese on each crepe. Lay the smoked salmon over the cheese and fold or roll the crepes. Lay in a buttered oven-proof dish, dot with butter, and reheat in a preheated 400° oven for 15 minutes. Serve with Bechamel sauce and garnish with smoked salmon rolls and sprigs of parsley.

salmon crepes

salmon crepes

Yield: 4 servings

2 tablespoons butter
2 tablespoons flour
¼ teaspoon salt
1 cup milk
1 small can pink or red salmon,
**   drained and flaked**
8 warm crepes
Optional extra: salad garnish

Melt butter in saucepan over low heat. Blend in flour and salt. Mix well. Add milk all at once. Cook over moderate heat, stirring constantly, until mixture thickens and bubbles. Add salmon; heat thoroughly. Spoon on crepes; roll up.

desserts

Crepes can be used to make a great variety of delicious desserts. Usually the sweeter dessert batters are used to make crepes for this purpose. The simplest crepe dessert is simply to provide a stack of dessert crepes and let the diners make their own. Put various jams or jellies in bowls; have one for confectioner's sugar, cinnamon, etc. If spontaneity is not appropriate to the meal, a number of attractive dessert recipes are available and some are given on the following pages.

blintzes

Yield: 4 servings

12 ounces cottage cheese
1 egg yolk
1 teaspoon butter, softened
1 teaspoon vanilla
18 crepes, cooked only on 1 side
2 teaspoons butter
2 teaspoons vegetable oil
2 tablespoons sugar
1 tablespoon cinnamon
Dairy sour cream to pass

Mix cheese, egg yolk, butter, and vanilla. Divide filling between the crepes on cooked side and roll up. Melt butter and oil in a large fry pan. Place half of crepes in pan and fry until golden brown, turning once. Repeat with rest of crepes. Add more butter and oil if necessary. Sprinkle each serving with sugar and cinnamon. Pass sour cream.

crepes with grape filling

Yield: 8 servings

4 cups blue grapes
¾ cup sugar
1½ tablespoons lemon juice
1 tablespoon grated orange rind
1 tablespoon quick-cooking
    tapioca
8 warm dessert crepes
Confectioner's sugar

Remove pulp from grape skins. Reserve skins and cook pulp until the seeds become loose. Press through a colander to remove seeds. Combine pulp and skins. Add sugar, lemon juice, orange rind and tapioca. Simmer for 20 minutes. Cool slightly and spread on warm dessert crepes. Roll up and sprinkle with the sugar.

Picture on previous page: dessert crepes

strawberry and orange crepes

Yield: 4 servings
  1 pint strawberries
  2 oranges
  2 tablespoons kirsch
  1 tablespoon Grand Marnier
  4 tablespoons red currant jelly
  8 dessert crepes
  2 tablespoons butter

Wash and slice the strawberries. Peel an orange and chop the peel into the smallest possible pieces. Put the peel in a saucepan of boiling water and simmer the peel for 15 minutes. Drain the peel. Cut the oranges into segments, cutting between the membranes.

Combine the sliced strawberries, orange segment, and peel. Sprinkle with 2 tablespoons kirsch and 1 tablespoon Grand Marnier. Spread each crepe with red currant jelly. Fill the crepes with 2 to 3 tablespoons combined fruits and roll into shape. Place the crepes in a buttered oven-proof dish and dot with butter. Bake in a preheated 400° oven for 15 minutes. Serve with a fruit sauce, lemon sauce or whipped cream.

mixed-fruit crepes with whipped cream

Yield: 6 servings
  3 bananas
  2 tablespoons heavy cream
  1 tablespoon sugar
  1 pound fresh or canned peaches
  1 pound fresh or canned pears
  12 dessert crepes
  2 tablespoons butter

Mash the bananas with cream and sugar and cover the surface of each crepe. Cut the peaches and pears into small pieces and lay over the bananas. Roll or fold the crepes. Place the crepes in a buttered oven-proof dish, dot with butter and bake in a preheated 400° oven for 15 minutes. Serve with a melba sauce or whipped cream.

puffy soufflé crepes

Yield: 6 servings

3 eggs, separated
1 cup milk
¾ cup flour
1 teaspoon sugar
¼ teaspoon salt
2 tablespoons butter, melted and
  slightly cooled
Strawberry or other fruit topping

Beat egg yolks with ½ cup milk. Add flour, sugar, and salt; beat well. Add rest of milk and melted butter. Beat egg whites until stiff peaks form and fold into crepe mixture. Cook as you would regular crepes or bake in a large greased pan in preheated oven (375°) for about 25 minutes. Top with sweetened sliced strawberries or other fruit.

puffy soufflé crepes

blueberry crepes

Yield: 6 servings
  2 pints blueberries
  ½ cup red wine
  ½ cup orange juice
  ¼ cup red currant jelly
  1 tablespoon arrowroot
  2 tablespoons cold water
  12 dessert crepes
  2 tablespoons butter
  Confectioner's sugar
  Whipped cream or sour cream

Wash the blueberries and put them in a bowl. Combine the wine, orange juice, and red currant jelly. Bring to the boiling point in a small saucepan. Dissolve 1 tablespoon arrowroot in 2 tablespoons cold water and add to the boiling liquid. It will thicken immediately. Remove from the heat and combine the sauce with the blueberries.

Put 2 to 3 tablespoons blueberries in each crepe. Roll the crepes and place in a buttered oven-proof dish. Dot the crepes with butter and bake in a preheated 400° oven. Cook for 15 minutes. When they are removed from the oven, dust the crepes heavily with sifted confectioner's sugar. Serve with whipped or sour cream.

fresh-fruit dessert crepes

Yield: 6 servings
  ½ cup commercial sour cream
  2 3-ounce packages of cream
      cheese, softened
  3 tablespoons sugar
  1 pint sliced strawberries or 2 cups
      sliced peaches
  12 dessert crepes

Blend sour cream, cream cheese, and sugar well; then whip until smooth and fluffy. Sweeten fruit with sugar and set aside. Top dessert crépe with 2 or 3 tablespoons of cream cheese mixture and roll up. Spoon fresh fruit over top. Serve cold or warm.

citrus crepes

Yield: 6 to 8 servings

12 small sugar cubes
1 orange
2 lemons
6 tablespoons butter
¾ cup Cointreau
16 warm dessert crepes
2 tablespoons sugar
Lemon slices for garnish

Rub sugar cubes over skin of orange to absorb oil. Squeeze orange and lemons; reserve juice. Melt 3 tablespoons butter in chafing dish. Drop in sugar cubes, and press to crush. Add rest of butter, juice, and ½ cup Cointreau. Heat, stirring, until well-mixed. Dip each crepe in sauce, and roll. Sprinkle with sugar. Add ¼ cup Cointreau and tilt pan toward flame to ignite. Garnish with lemon slices

citrus crepes

black-cherry crepes

Yield: 4 servings

**2 pounds pitted black Bing
    cherries
¼ teaspoon ground cinnamon
¼ cup sugar
Rind and juice of 2 oranges
1 tablespoon kirsch
1 teaspoon arrowroot
8 dessert crepes
2 tablespoons confectioner's sugar
1 tablespoon butter
Toasted almonds or whipped
    cream**

Drain the cherries and reserve the juice. Simmer the cherries in a covered saucepan over moderately low heat with the cinnamon, sugar and orange rind. There will be enough juice still clinging to the cherries to prevent them from burning. Dissolve the arrowroot in the orange juice and add to the pan of hot cherries and continue cooking until a thick sauce is formed around the cherries. Add 1 tablespoon kirsch. If the sauce appears too thin, add another teaspoon arrowroot dissolved first in 1 tablespoon reserved cherry juice. If the sauce is too thick, thin it out a little with more juice. Butter an oven-proof dish. Put 2 tablespoons of the cherry filling in each crepe and roll the crepe. Dot the surface of the crepes with 1 tablespoon butter and heat in a preheated oven at 400° for 15 minutes.

Sprinkle the surface of the heated crepes with sifted confectioner's sugar and serve with toasted almonds over the confectioner's sugar or with whipped cream.

apricot soufflé crepes

Yield: 6 servings

2 cups dried apricots
1 cup water
6 eggs, separated
⅔ cup sugar

2 cups egg custard or 1 package egg
    custard mix
Slivered toasted almonds
12 warm dessert crepes

Prepare apricot purée by simmering apricots in water until tender. Sieve or purée in blender. Reserve.

Beat egg yolks and sugar until thick. In separate bowl, beat egg whites until stiff. Fold ½ cup apricot purée into beaten yolks and fold this mixture into egg whites.

Spread crepes with a little of the remaining apricot purée, then divide egg mixture between crepes. Lightly fold crepes over soufflé and place in baking dish. Cook in very hot oven (450°) for 4 minutes or until puffy. Pour warm custard over crepes; sprinkle with almonds and serve.

apricot soufflé crepes

apple crepes with roquefort cheese

Yield: 4 servings
  2 pounds cooking apples
  2 tablespoons butter
  1 tablespoon sugar
  ½ pound Roquefort cheese
  1 to 2 tablespoons heavy cream
  8 dessert crepes
  1 tablespoon butter

Peel, core, and cut the apples into thin slices. Melt 2 tablespoons butter in a frying pan. Add the apples. Sprinkle the apples with sugar and cook until the apples are lightly browned but not soft.

Put the cheese in a bowl; add the cream and work into a paste, using the back of a wooden spoon.

Spread out the crepes and cover the surface of each crepe with the Roquefort cheese. Put 1 to 2 tablespoons sautéed apple slices in each crepe and roll or fold the crepes into envelopes.

Lay the crepes on a buttered oven-proof dish, dot with 1 tablespoon butter and bake in preheated 400° oven for 15 minutes. Decorate the dish with apple slices. 1

sour cream-strawberries crepes

Yield: 8 servings
  2 cups commercial sour cream
  4 tablespoons sugar
  1 pint sliced strawberries
  1 tablespoon butter
  16 dessert crepes
  Powdered sugar

Blend sour cream and sugar. Roll up crepes with a filling of 1 tablespoon sour cream mixture and 1 tablespoon strawberries. Refrigerate, covered, until serving time. In pan or blazing pan of chafing dish melt butter over direct high flame. Turn crepes to heat evenly. Add strawberries; heat. Sprinkle with powdered sugar.

tangy apple crepes

Yield: 4 servings
3 tablespoons margarine
5 medium tangy apples, peeled,
      cored and sliced ½ inch thick
1½ tablespoons lemon juice
¾ teaspoon lemon peel
¼ teaspoon cinnamon
⅛ teaspoon allspice
½ cup sugar
8 crepes

Melt margarine over medium heat in a large pan. Gently cook apples, mixed with lemon juice, peel, and spices about 8 minutes or until apples are just tender. Cook 2 to 3 minutes longer after sprinkling with sugar. Cool to room temperature.

Roll up about 3 tablespoons filling in crepes and place seam side down in baking dish. Cover with remaining filling. Tightly cover dish with foil and bake at 325° for about 25 minutes.

apricot crepes with marmalade sauce

Yield: 4 servings
2 pounds fresh or canned apricots
(1 cup water combined with 1 cup
      sugar)
Pinch of cloves (optional)
Pinch of cinnamon (optional)
Grated lemon peel from 1 lemon
Juice of half a lemon
8 dessert crepes
2 tablespoons butter
2 tablespoons confectioner's sugar

If fresh apricots are used, poach the fruit for 8 minutes in a simple syrup made by combining 1 cup of water with 1 cup of sugar.

Drain the apricots and cut into smaller pieces. A pinch of cloves and cinnamon may be added to the apricots if you like. Sprinkle apricots with lemon juice and grated lemon peel. Spread out the crepes and fill each with 2 tablespoons apricots. Lay the crepes in a buttered oven-proof dish. Dot the surface with butter. Bake in a preheated oven at 400° for 15 minutes. Sprinkle the crepes heavily with confectioner's sugar, when they are removed from the oven. Serve with marmalade sauce or whipped cream.

three easy dessert crepes

Prepare dessert crepes ahead and warm in a 300° oven for 10 minutes. Use your imagination for filling and garnishing the crepes.

crepes with applesauce

Fill crepes with applesauce mixed with whipped cream. Garnish with ground cinnamon.

crepes with preserves

Fill crepes with strawberry or raspberry jam. Lingonberry preserves are also very delicious and attractive. Garnish with the same preserve or with sugar.

crepes with marmalade and pecans

Fill with equal amounts of chopped pecans and orange marmalade. Roll and sprinkle with sugar.

Picture on next page: 3 easy dessert crepes

(top to bottom)

crepes with applesauce
crepes with preserves
crepes with marmalade and pecans

banana crepes

Yield: 8 servings
- ⅓ **cup butter**
- ½ **cup orange marmalade**
- 2 **tablespoons sugar**
- 1 **tablespoon cornstarch**
- 3 **large bananas, sliced**
- 2 **tablespoons confectioner's sugar**
- **Nutmeg, if desired**
- 8 **warm dessert crepes**

Heat butter and marmalade until the marmalade melts. In a separate container mix sugar and cornstarch. Gradually stir into butter-marmalade mixture. Cook over medium heat, stirring constantly, until mixture bubbles. Remove from heat and gently stir in bananas. Divide between warm crepes and roll. Sprinkle tops with confectioner's sugar and nutmeg, if desired.

strawberry-banana crepes

Yield: 8 servings
- ¾ **cup water**
- 2 **cups strawberries, crushed**
- 2 **cups strawberries, halved**
- ¼ **cup sugar**
- 2 **tablespoons cornstarch**
- ½ **cup Curacao or other orange liqueur**
- 3 **medium bananas, quartered**
- 8 **warm dessert crepes**

In a medium saucepan add ¾ cup water to 2 cups crushed strawberries. Bring to a boil and cook 2 minutes. Strain. Combine sugar and cornstarch and gradually stir into hot strawberry mixture. Cook over medium heat, stirring constantly, until mixture thickens and bubbles. Remove from heat. Stir in liqueur and set aside 1 cup of glaze. Stir half of the strawberry halves into remaining glaze. Spread 3 tablespoons glaze on each crepe and roll up. Place in chafing dish or large fry pan with the rest of strawberry halves and quartered bananas. Pour reserved glaze over top; cover and heat through. Serve warm.

strawberry cream crepes

Yield: 6 servings
 4 cups fresh strawberries, sliced
 2 tablespoons sugar
 **1 14-ounce can sweetened
  condensed milk**
 ¼ cup lemon juice
 ½ cup heavy cream, whipped
 12 dessert crepes
 Whipped cream for garnish
 12 whole strawberries for garnish

Sprinkle strawberries with sugar and set aside. Beat condensed milk with lemon juice until thick. Fold in strawbewries and whipped cream. Divide between crepes and fold. Garnish with additional whipped cream and a strawberry centered on cream.

chocolate and nut crepes

Yield: 6 servings
 2 tablespoons cocoa
 ⅓ cup cornstarch
 ¼ cup sugar
 2½ cups milk
 ½ cup chopped walnuts
 6 warm dessert crepes

Blend the cocoa, cornstarch, and sugar with a small amount of milk. Bring the rest of the milk to a boil and blend into cocoa mixture. Return to the pan and bring to a boil, stirring constantly, until thick. Reserve ¼ cup of the chocolate sauce and 1 tablespoon of the chopped walnuts. Mix the rest of the sauce with the nuts. Fill warm crepes with the mixture and roll up. Spoon the remaining sauce on top of crepes and sprinkle with reserved nuts. Serve at once.

cream cheese and raisin crepes

Yield: 6 servings
  1/3 cup yellow raisins
  1/4 cup boiling water
  8-ounce package cream cheese,
      softened
  1/4 cup sugar
  3 small lemons, sliced
  6 warm dessert crepes

Soak raisins in a bowl with 1/4 cup boiling water for 10 minutes. Drain. Mix the cream cheese and sugar with the raisins. Make crepes. Spoon mixture into the center of each pancake. Roll up; serve decorated with lemon slices.

mandarin-cream crepes

Yield: 6 servings
  2 small cans mandarin oranges
  3 tablespoons apricot jam, sieved
  1/2 cup heavy cream
  Candy orange slices
  6 warm dessert crepes

Drain mandarin oranges; mix them with jam. Lightly whip the cream until thick but not buttery. Place in a pastry bag with small star nozzle. Spoon mandarin mixture into the center of each crepe and roll up. Pipe a line of cream on each pancake and decorate with candy orange slices.

Picture on next page: (top to bottom)

cream cheese and raisin crepes
madarin-cream crepes
peach dessert crepes
chocolate and nut crepes
cherry and apple crepes

peach dessert crepes

Yield: 6 servings
**2 16-ounce cans sliced peaches
1 15- to 16-ounce can red cherries
¼ cup golden syrup
6 warm dessert crepes**

Drain fruit. Set aside 15 cherries and 15 peach slices. Cut these cherries in half and slice peaches. Chop rest of fruit. Mix chopped fruit with syrup. Warm mixture on low heat. Fill warm crepes with mixture and roll up. Decorate.

cherry and apple crepes

Yield: 6 servings
**6 cooking apples
¾ cup sugar
⅛ teaspoon cinnamon
¼ cup water
1 16-ounce can cherry pie filling
½ cup sugar
6 warm rich dessert crepes**

Peel, core, and slice the apples. Place in a pan with the ¾ cup sugar, cinnamon and ¼ cup water. Cover and cook over a low heat for 15 minutes or until the apples are just cooked. Heat the cherry pie filling. Drain apples and spoon apples into the center of each crepe. Spoon pie filling at each end. Carefully roll up each crepe. Sprinkle on ½ cup sugar. Heat 2 skewers over gas or electric burner until very hot. Using an oven mitt to hold skewer, place a skewer diagonally over the sugared crepes. Repeat with the second skewer, placing it at the opposite angle. Repeat until all the crepes are decorated in this way. Serve at once while crepes are hot. For a special occasion, serve with whipped cream.

fruity crepes

Yield: 6 servings
1 package mincemeat
½ cup orange juice
2 tablespoons orange marmalade
1 tablespoon grape jam or jelly
12 warm dessert crepes

Cook mincemeat according to package directions except substitute orange juice for ½ cup water. Add marmalade and jelly. If possible, refrigerate overnight to blend flavors. Fill each crepe with mincemeat and roll up. Serve hot with whipped cream.

fruity crepes

baked-apple crepe cake

Yield: 6 servings
  **2 pounds apples, sliced (about 6
      medium apples)**
  ⅓ cup sugar
  ¼ cup melted butter
  12 crepes
  6 stale macaroons, crumbled
  1 tablespoon melted butter
  1 tablespoon sugar

Spread apples in a baking pan and sprinkle with sugar and butter. Cook at 350° for 15 minutes or until apples are tender. Place 2 crepes side by side in a greased baking dish and spread with layers of apple slices and sprinkle with macaroons. Place 2 crepes on top and continue with apple filling. Top with crepes. Brush with melted butter and sprinkle with sugar. Bake at 375° until bubbly.

apple strudel crepes

Yield: 6 servings
  1 16-ounce can applesauce
  12 dessert crepes
  ½ cup butter
  2 tablespoons sugar
  3 tablespoons confectioner's sugar
  2 teaspoons cinnamon

Spread applesauce over each crepe and roll up. Melt butter in a hot frying pan or chafing dish. Place crepes in pan or chafing dish and brush tops with butter. Sprinkle with 2 tablespoons sugar. Heat until lightly browned on all sides. Sprinkle with confectioner's sugar and cinnamon. Serve.

cream of almond crepes

Yield: 6 servings

12 to 15 dessert crepes
2 tablespoons butter
2 tablespoons flour
1 cup milk
3 ounces almond extract
3 eggs yolks
1 cup sugar
½ teaspoon salt
¼ cup Grand Marnier liqueur or
  rum

Melt butter and blend in flour. Cook for 1 minute and add cold milk. Bring to a simmer and cook 2 to 3 minutes, stirring constantly. Remove from heat. Add almond extract, egg yolks, sugar and salt. Beat. Adjust sweetness to your taste and add the Grand Marnier liqueur. Refrigerate until cold. Divide the mixture between the crepes and roll up package style. Place crepes in an oven-proof dish and dot with butter. Sprinkle tops with sugar. Place under broiler for 3 to 4 minutes, until sugar is browned.

cream of almond crepes
russian crepes

russian crepes

Yield: 6 servings
12 warm dessert crepes
¾ cup cottage cheese
½ cup sugar
Pinch of cardamom
2 eggs, separated
¼ teaspoon salt
⅓ cup candied cherries, chopped
4 egg whites
⅓ cup raisins
⅓ cup candied orange peel,
   chopped
1 tablespoon lemon peel

Drain the cottage cheese. Mix with the sugar, egg yolks, cardamom, and salt until it resembles a thick paste. Add all the fruit, including the lemon peel. Whip the 6 egg whites to stiff peaks and fold into cheese mixture. Divide the mixture between the crepes and roll up. Place in oven-proof dish and sprinkle a little sugar over the tops. Place under broiler for 3 to 4 minutes to brown sugar and warm filling. Serve immediately.

date-nut crepes

Yield: 8 servings
1 cup chopped dates
1 cup chopped pecans
½ cup light-brown sugar
1 cup dairy sour cream
8 warm dessert crepes

Mix dates, pecans, brown sugar, and sour cream. Fill and roll up or allow guests to help themselves.

crepe gateau

Yield: Approximately 6 servings

24 to 30 dessert crepes
applesauce
Various preserves and jams of
your choice: blackberry,
orange marmalade,
gooseberry,   raspberry,
strawberry, grape, etc.
Custard
Fruit-flavored liqueur

Stack the dessert crepes one at a time and place a layer of applesauce, custard, or preserve between each 2 crepes. Top with the liqueur and cut into quarters with a sharp knife.

crepe gateau

danish prune crepes

Yield: 4 servings
¾ cup dried prunes
3 tablespoons sugar
¼ teaspoon ground cardamom
½ teaspoon vanilla
⅛ teaspoon salt
4 warm dessert crepes
2 tablespoons confectioner's sugar

Add enough water to cover prunes. Bring to a boil; then reduce heat and simmer, covered, for 30 minutes. Drain prunes, reserving 3 tablespoons liquid. Cool, pit and chop. Combine prunes, prune liquid, sugar, and cardamom. Cook, stirring continuously, for 5 minutes or until mixture is thick. Add vanilla and salt.

Divide between warm crepes and roll. Sprinkle with sugar and serve.

george washington crepes

Yield: 8 servings
2 cups sour cream
4 tablespoons sugar
1 teaspoon almond extract
1 can cherry pie filling
16 dessert crepes
2 tablespoons butter

Blend sour cream, sugar, and almond extract. Spoon 1 tablespoon sour cream mixture and 1 tablespoon pie filling on each crepe; roll up. Cover and refrigerate until serving time. When ready to serve, melt butter in blazing pan of chafing dish over direct high heat. Heat crepe, turning to heat evenly. Spoon remaining pie filling over crepes; heat carefully to avoid scorching, and serve.

lemon dessert crepes

Yield: 6 servings
3 tablespoons sweet butter
4 tablespoons unsifted all-purpose
    flour
½ cup hot milk
3 eggs, separated
3 tablespoons sugar
3 tablespoons lemon juice
1 teaspoon dried lemon peel
Salt
12 dessert crepes

Preheat oven to 400°. Melt butter over low heat, blend in flour, and continue cooking and stirring 1 to 2 minutes. Remove from heat and beat in milk. Return to heat and stir continuously until mixture boils and thickens. Transfer to a bowl before beating in egg yolks one at a time. Stirring thoroughly, blend in 3 tablespoons sugar, lemon juice, and lemon peel. In another bowl, whip egg whites with ⅛ teaspoon salt until they form soft peaks; continue beating until whites form stiff peaks. Gently fold in a small amount of whites to lemon mixture; then add remaining whites to the mixture.

Add 1 tablespoon of lemon mixture on dessert crepe and fold the crepes in half and in half again. Place in shallow, buttered baking dish side by side, and bake 10 minutes.

whipped-cream filled crepes

Yield: 6 servings
½ pint heavy cream, chilled
Sugar and vanilla to taste
1 pint fresh raspberries or
    strawberries
6 warm dessert crepes

Whip chilled cream until thick. Add sugar and vanilla to taste. Divide whipping cream between crepes; fill and roll. Garnish with berries and sprinkle sugar over tops for a beautiful but simple dessert. (A filling of sour cream would be a delicious variation.)

chocolate-coconut crepes

Yield: 8 servings
    8 ounces sweet chocolate
    ½ cup water
    1 tablespoon butter
    ½ cup heavy cream
    1 cup coconut
    8 crepes

Melt chocolate, water, and butter over low heat. Slowly mix in cream to make sauce. Stir in coconut. Divide between crepes and roll up.

hot-fudge crepes

Yield: 6 servings
    ½ cup butter
    1 cup sugar
    1 teaspoon instant coffee powder
    2 tablespoons rum
    ⅓ cup cocoa
    1 cup heavy cream
    1 teaspoon vanilla
    12 crepes
    12 small scoops chocolate ice
        cream
Whipped cream for garnish

Melt butter in saucepan and blend in sugar, coffee powder, rum, and cocoa. Add cream and heat to simmer temperature. Cook about 5 minutes, stirring occasionally. Remove from heat and add vanilla. Fill crepes with ice cream and pour fudge sauce over filled crepes. Top with whipped cream.

Picture on previous page: whipped-cream-filled crepes

hot ice cream crepes

...ngs
... crepes
... cream
... sauce

...Divide ice cream between the crepes and roll up. Place in
...hot oven for about 2 to 3 minutes. Serve with cold
ch...

hot ice cream crepes

BUTTERSCOTCH FUDGE
(25 pieces)

1½ cups sugar
½ cup butter
1 can (5.33 ounces) evaporated milk
1 package (6 ounces) butterscotch pieces
1 cup marshmallow creme
½ teaspoon vanilla
½ cup coarsely chopped walnuts or pecans
pecan halves for garnish

Combine sugar, butter and milk in 3-quart casserole. Microcook on high 8 to 10 minutes, stirring several times, until candy thermometer reaches 230°. Stir in butterscotch pieces, marshmallow creme and vanilla until blended. Stir in nuts. Pour into buttered 9-inch round glass dish. Immediately press pecan halves into top of fudge in decorative pattern, if you wish.

ice cream crepes with raspberry sauce

Yield: 8 servings
  1 10-ounce package frozen
      raspberries
  ½ cup sugar
  1 tablespoon cornstarch
  ¼ teaspoon nutmeg
  1 tablespoon lemon juice
  8 crepes
  Vanilla ice cream
  ½ cup whipped cream

Thaw berries. In a saucepan combine sugar, cornstarch, and nutmeg. Stir in berries and lemon juice. Cook, stirring, until thickened. Cool 5 to 10 minutes. Fill crepes with ice cream. Fold over and spoon warm sauce over tops. Garnish with whipped cream.

fondue chips

Yield: 4 to 6 servings
  6 dessert crepes
  Powdered sugar

Cut each crepe into 12 or 16 pieces. Place on a cookie sheet and bake at 400° for 6 to 8 minutes or until crisp. Remove from oven and sprinkle with sugar. Use with chocolate fondue.

chocolate fondue

Yield: 4 to 6 servings
  10 ounces milk chocolate
  ½ cup heavy cream
  2 tablespoons kirsch or cognac

Break chocolate into pieces about 1 inch square and combine with other ingredients in fondue pot over low heat. Stir until chocolate is melted and mixture is smooth. Dip fondue chips into sauce.

crepes with chocolate mousse

Yield: 8 servings
- **6 ounces semisweet chocolate pieces**
- **1 teaspoon sugar**
- **1 teaspoon vanilla**
- **⅓ cup boiling water**
- **4 eggs, separated**
- **8 dessert crepes**
- **Whipped cream to garnish**

In a blender grind chocolate pieces until powdery; loosen pieces from corners so all chocolate is ground. Add sugar, vanilla and boiling water and blend until chocolate is smooth. Add the egg yolks to blending chocolate. Beat the egg whites until stiff peaks are formed. Fold chocolate into whites and blend. Chill at least 1 hour before filling crepes. Divide mixture between crepes and roll. Garnish tops with whipped cream.

meringue crepes

Yield: 6 servings
- **4 egg whites**
- **¾ cup sugar**
- **½ cup and 2 tablespoons Cointreau or orange liqueur**
- **½ cup chopped almonds**
- **16 crepes**

Beat egg whites until soft peaks are formed. Slowly beat in sugar until whites are stiff. Fold in 2 tablespoons Cointreau or orange liqueur. Divide meringue between crepes, sprinkle with 1 tablespoon almonds, and roll up. Place in heated serving pan. Sprinkle with rest of almonds. Add ½ cup Cointreau, warm and ignite. Spoon over crepes.

brandied apricot crepes

Yield: 4 to 6 servings
- **12 dessert crepes**
- **½ cup apricot jam**
- **3 tablespoons sugar**
- **2 tablespoons melted butter**
- **⅓ cup apricot brandy**

Spread jam over crepes. Roll up and arrange in buttered baking dish. Sprinkle with sugar and melted butter. Broil for a minute or two to brown tops. Heat brandy in a small pan. Pour over crepes and ignite with long match. Serve.

peach-nut flambé

Yield: 4 servings
- **⅓ cup butter**
- **1 16-ounce can sliced peaches**
- **½ cup chopped pecans**
- **1 teaspoon grated orange peel**
- **1 tablespoon sugar**
- **¼ cup brandy**
- **8 warm dessert crepes**

Melt butter in chafing dish. Drain peaches and pour juice into pan with butter. Simmer about 5 minutes. Stir in peaches and pecans. Sprinkle with orange peel and sugar. Warm brandy in a small pan and add. Ignite with a long match. Spoon sauce over crepes.

coffee crepes flambé

Yield: 6 servings
12 crepes
¼ cup brown sugar, packed
⅛ teaspoon cinnamon
⅓ cup heavy cream
6 tablespoons coffee-flavored
**   liqueur, heated**
Whipped cream for garnish

Fold crepes in quarters. In chafing dish combine brown sugar, cinnamon, and cream. Heat to simmer, stirring continuously. Add folded crepes and coat with sauce. With a long match, ignite liqueur. Pour into chafing dish while flaming and spoon over crepes. Garnish with whipped cream before serving.

flaming crepes d' angers

Yield: 8 servings
1 cup heavy cream
½ cup and 2 tablespoons orange
**   liqueur**
2 tablespoons sugar
Grated semisweet chocolate
16 crepes

Whip cream and add 2 tablespoons orange liqueur. Fold crepes in quarters and arrange in heated serving pan. Sprinkle with sugar. Add ½ cup orange liqueur, warm, and ignite. Spoon liqueur over crepes. Top each crepe with whipped cream and a sprinkle of chocolate.

crepes suzettes

Yield: 6 servings
- **6 cubes of sugar**
- **2 oranges**
- **1 lemon**
- **1 stick soft sweet butter**
- **¼ cup Grand Marnier, Curacao, Benedictine, Cointreau or Triple Sec**
- **12 dessert crepes**
- **¼ cup brandy**

Rub 6 cubes of sugar over the rind of the oranges and lemon and combine it on a plate with 1 stick of soft sweet butter.

Place the flavored butter in the chafing dish and add the juice of 1 orange and 1 lemon and ¼ cup of one of the above liqueurs.

When the contents of the pan are hot and bubbling, add the crepes one at a time. Coat each crepe with the sauce, fold it into a triangle, and push it to the side of the dish. When all the crepes are coated with sauce, arrange them over the surface of the dish and allow them to heat through. Flame the crepes with ¼ cup brandy and serve immediately.

Picture on next page: crepes suzettes

easy crepes suzettes

Yield: 6 servings

½ cup sweet butter, softened
¼ cup sugar
2 teaspoons orange peel, grated
½ cup orange juice
¼ cup curacao
1 small orange, sliced
1 small lemon, sliced
2 tablespoons brandy
12 warm dessert crepes

Cream butter and beat in sugar. Add orange peel, juice, and curacao. Spread orange butter on each crepe. Fold into fourths. Decorate with orange and lemon slices. Pour brandy over and serve. (If flaming dessert is desired, heat brandy in small pan, pour over crepes and ignite.)

Picture on next page: easy crepes suzettes

stacked crepes suzettes

Yield: 4 servings
- ½ **pound unsalted butter,**
  softened
- ½ **cup sugar**
- **1 teaspoon lemon juice**
- ½ **cup orange juice**
- ¼ **cup orange liqueur**
- **16 dessert crepes**
- **1 tablespoon sugar**
- **2 tablespoons orange liqueur**
- **2 tablespoons cognac**

Beat butter with ½ cup sugar until thoroughly mixed. Add lemon juice, orange juice and ¼ cup liqueur while continuing to beat. Heat orange butter until bubbly. Dip crepes in hot orange butter and stack. Sprinkle top with 1 tablespoon sugar. Heat liqueur and cognac. Pour over stacked crepes and ignite. Spoon sauce over crepes until flames die. Cut and serve immediately.

stacked crepes suzette

crepes suzettes with almonds

Yield: 6 servings
  2 tablespoons butter
  2 tablespoons confectioner's sugar
  Rind and juice from 1 lemon
  1½ ounces orange liqueur or
      Grand Marnier, rouge
  2 tablespoons almonds, chopped
  1½ ounces brandy or Grand
      Marnier for flaming
  12 warm dessert crepes

Cream butter and mix in sugar, lemon rind, juice, 1½ ounces orange liqueur, and almonds. Fold crepes in fourths and spread with orange butter. Place in an oven-proof pan. Add rest of sauce on top of crepes. Place in a hot oven (400°) for a few minutes to heat. Warm brandy or Grand Marnier, pour over crepes, and flame at the table.

crepes suzettes with almonds

entertaining with crepes

Breakfasts and brunches are easy ways to entertain guests. Keep the menu light—only one main dish is necessary. Crepe dishes look difficult, but most are simple. They can be prepared well in advance. Add a garnish, juice, and coffee for the easiest possible meal. These same meals could be served in the evening as suppers or late evening snacks.

crepe breakfast

Orange Juice
Crepes with Ham Quiche*
Coffee   Milk

This crepe can be prepared the night before and served cold, or warmed in a 300°F oven. It is a nutritious breakfast and different from the usual bacon and eggs.

make-ahead brunch

Fresh Fruit Ambrosia
Smoked Salmon and Cream Cheese Crepes*
Cinnamon Coffee Cake
Coffee

These easy brunch foods can be made a day ahead and heated after the guests arrive. Simple and delicious!

patio brunch

Chilled Melon Balls with Strawberries
Omelette with Cheese Sauce
Ham-Filled Crepes*
Coffee

Let the fruit course double as a centerpiece and serve it as a last course. Prepare crepes and cheese sauce ahead but cook omelette just before serving.

special-occasion brunch

Cheese and Pineapple Skewers
Curried-Crab Crepes*
Chicken Livers in White Wine
Apricot Crepes*   Stuffed Eggs   Coffee
This menu provides a brunch that is easy to prepare yet elegant.

*Recipe included in book

130

other suggestions for brunch:

Chicken-Liver Crepes in Madeira Sauce*
Crepes with Welsh Rarebit Sauce*
Mushroom-Ham Crepes*
Mushroom Crepes with Ham*
Ham and Asparagus Crepes*
Salmon Crepes*

luncheons featuring crepes
oriental luncheon

Chicken Consommé with Crepes*

Beef and Snow Peas Crepes*
Cucumber Salad

Fortune Cookies   Green Tea

Although this luncheon has several courses, it stays well within a modest calorie count.

bridge-party luncheon

Ham and Asparagus Crepes*
Crisp Green Salad   French Dressing

Black-Cherry Crepes*   Coffee

Greet your guests in a relaxed manner by serving this crepe luncheon. All foods can be prepared ahead and heated in the oven. Add suggested garnishes and serve.

other luncheon suggestions

French Onion Soup with Crepes*
Bouillon with Crepes*
Smoked Oyster Crepes*
Crabby Crepes*
Curried-Crab Appetizers*
Crepes with Bacon Quiche*
Crepes with Ham Quiche*
Egg and Zucchini Crepes*
Asparagus and Egg Crepes*
Chicken-Liver Crepes in Madeira Sauce*

*Recipe included in book

Cheese, Bacon, and Onion Crepes*
Ham and Beef Crepes*
Crepes with Swedish Meatballs*
Beef and Blue Cheese Crepes*
Crepes with Hamburger Stroganoff*
Cheese Layer Crepes*
Mushroom-Ham Crepes*
Ham-Filled Crepes*
Spinach and Ham Crepes*
Easy Turkey-Spinach Crepes*
Crepes with Cashew-Chicken Filling*
Quick Chicken Divan Crepes*
Crepes with Hot Chicken Salad*
Elsa's Chicken Crepe Soufflé*
Cannelloni Crepes*
Manicotti*
Hawaiian Crepes*
Beef and Bean Sprout Crepes*
Shrimp and Water Chestnut Crepes*
Shrimp Crepes with Veloute Sauce*
Crab-Filled Crepewich*
Crab Crepes with Tomatoes and Herbs*
Creamed-Crab in Crepes*
Creamed-Oyster Crepes*
Chicken and Oyster Crepes*
Crispy Tuna-Noodle Crepes*
Tuna with Herbs Crepes*
Crepes Romaine*
Smoked Salmon and Cream Cheese Crepes*
Salmon Crepes*

vegetarian luncheons

These menus provide an interesting variety of foods that supply necessary complete protein. Don't be at a loss when vegetarian friends come for lunch.

Crepes with Fresh Mushrooms*
Greens with Papaya
Assorted Cheeses
Toasted Pumpernickel Bread

Mandarin-Cream Crepes*
Coffee

*Recipe included in book

Asparagus and Egg Crepes*
Stuffed Summer Squash
Breadsticks

Ice Cream Crepes with Raspberry Sauce*
Coffee

other meatless crepes
Crepes Madrilene*
Egg and Zucchini Crepes*
Green Beans in Cheese Crepes*
Cauliflower Crepes with Mornay Sauce*
Creamed-Mushroom Crepes*
Ratatouille Crepes*
Green Crepes*
Crepes with Welsh Rarebit Sauce*
Crepes with Cottage Cheese*

elegant cocktail party
Crepes with Caviar*
Liver Paté   Assorted Crackers
Smoked Oyster Crepes*
Fresh Vegetables with Dip
Curried-Crab Appetizers*
Tiny Cream Puffs with Chicken Salad

Prepare all foods ahead. When necessary, keep them warm or reheat to serve. Make use of electric warming trays and chafing dishes for keeping the crepes warm. These foods can be eaten with the fingers. A small plate may be used in addition to napkins. Punch or cocktails would accompany food.

cocktail appetizers
Chili-Blue Cheese Crepes*
Cheesy Dipping Chips*
Cheese-Olive Snack*
Appetizer Wedges*
Crepes with Fillings*
Tuna Paté Crepes*
Crabby Crepes*
Curried-Crab Appetizers*
Crepes with Caviar*
Deviled-Crab Crepes*
Cheese and Beef Rolls*
Deviled-Ham Crepes*
Dried-Beef Appetizers*   *Recipe included in book

133

crepe dinners

easy company dinner

Chicken-FilledCrepes*
Tossed Greens with Grapefruit Sections
Citrus Dressing
Baked Tomatoes

Crepes with Chocolate Mousse*
Coffee

If you don't know your guests' food preferences, use this easy plan with traditional foods.

guest dinner italian style

Antipasto Salad
Manicotti*
Marinated Artichoke Hearts
Garlic French Bread

Assorted Fresh Fruits and Cheese
Coffee

This informal menu could be served equally well on the patio or inside.

dinner-party entrées

Curried-Lamb Crepes*
Beef Stroganoff Crepes*
Beef Burgundy Crepes*
Crepes with Veal*
Crepes Saint Rafael*
Crepes with Cashew-Chicken Filling*
Chicken in White Wine Crepes*
Chicken-Filled Crepes*
Elsa's Chicken Crepe Soufflé*
Hawaiian Crepes*
Beef and Snow Peas Crepes*
Oriental Beef and Pepper Crepes*
Beef and Bean Sprout Crepes*
China Crepes*
Shrimp and Water Chestnut Crepes*
Shrimp Crepes with Veloute Sauce*
Creamed-Crab in Crepes*
Chicken and Oyster Crepes*
Down-East Lobster Crepes*

*Recipe included in book

continental dinner

French Onion Soup with Crepes*

Beef Stroganoff Crepes*
Buttered French-Style Green Beans
Fresh Fruit Salad

Apricot-Soufflé Crepes*
Coffee

Use your nicest table appointments for this formal dinner.

first-course suggestions

French Onion Soup with Crepes*
Bouillon with Crepes*
Chicken Consommé with Crepes*
Smoked Oyster Crepes*
Crepes with Bacon Quiche*
Crepes with Ham Quiche*
Crepes with Chicken Liver Paté*

an informal buffet

Chilled Relishes
Assorted Cold Meats
Crepes with Bacon Quiche*
Mandarin Orange Salad
Hot Rolls   Butter

Stacked Crepes Suzette*
Coffee

Serve quiche hot and if necessary keep warm on a warming tray. Let guests help themselves. Main-course foods should be cleared and replaced by dessert items. Flame crepes with guests watching.

flaming desserts

Meringue Crepes*
Crepes Suzettes*
Stacked Crepes Suzettes*
Easy Crepes Suzettes*
Crepe Suzettes with Almonds*
Brandied Apricot Crepes*
Coffee Crepes Flambe*
Flaming Crepes d' Angers*
Peach-Nut Flambé*

*Recipe included in book

crepes and dieting

Crepes are low in calories and conveniently package one's food in easy-to-measure portions. Overeating without being aware of it becomes more difficult. The creative expression involved in crepe cookery helps to relieve psychological frustration. The life-style evidenced in creative cookery is incompatible with the sedentary way of life often associated with obesity. It should be remembered, however, that many crepe fillings are not low in calories and are often topped with rich sauces. Vegetable and fruit crepes are generally lowest in calories. Poultry crepes tend to be lowest in calories among the meat dishes. Although regular crepe batters are low in calories, for the weight conscious there are batters that are even lower in calories and particularly designed for controlling weight. Filling will have to be selected with some care if weight-control is your objective.

calorie-counters crepe batter

Yield: 18 to 22 crepes

3 eggs
1 cup flour
¼ cup instant nonfat dry milk
1 cup water
⅛ teaspoon salt

Combine ingredients in medium mixing bowl. Beat with electric mixer, blend in a blender, or whisk until smooth. Refrigerate 1 hour or more. If batter separates, stir gently before cooking. Cook on upside-down crepe griddle or in traditional pan.

the energy content of some crepe fillings

Ingredient	Household Measure	kcals
Chopped, shelled almonds	1 cup	777
	1 tablespoon	48
Apple sauce, unsweetened	1 cup	100
sweetened	1 cup	232
Apple slices	1 cup	60
Cooked asparagus	4 spears	16
Raw avocados	1 avocado	378
Cooked bacon	2 slices, thick	143
	medium	86
	thin	61
Raw bananas	1 banana	100
Cooked bean sprouts	1 cup	35
Cooked boneless beef, diced	1 cup	458
Raw ground beef	1 cup	405
Cooked beet slices	1 cup	54
Raw blackberries	1 cup	84
Raw blueberries	1 cup	90
Cooked bluefish	1 fillet, baked	246
	fried	400
Shelled Brazil nuts	1 cup	916
Cooked broccoli	1 stalk, large	73
	medium	47
	small	36
Cooked Brussels sprouts	1 cup	56
Cooked carrot slices	1 cup	48
Roasted cashew nuts	1 cup	785
Cooked cauliflower	1 cup	28
Blue cheese, crumbled	1 cup	497
Cheddar cheese, shredded	1 cup	450
Cream cheese	1 cup	868
Swiss cheese	1 slice	130
Cherries, sweet	10 cherries	47

Ingredient	Household Measure	kcals
Chicken, roasted and diced	1 cup	232
Chocolate syrup	2 tablespoons	92
Cooked cod	1 fillet	111
Cooked collards	1 cup	42
Cottage cheese	1 cup	239
Cooked crab meat	1 cup	144
Heavy whipping cream	1 tablespoon	53
Light whipping cream	1 tablespoon	45
Eggs	1 egg, extra large	94
	large	82
	medium	72
Raw figs	1 fig	50
Filberts	10 nuts	87
Baked flounder	1 fillet	115
Frankfurters	1 frankfurter	139
Goose	3 ounces	198
Seedless grapes	10 grapes	34
Fried haddock	1 fillet	182
Cooked ham, chopped	1 cup	524
Ice cream	1 cup	257
Jams, sweetened	1 tablespoon	57
Jellies, sweetened	1 tablespoon	51
Cooked kale	1 cup	43
Roasted lamb, diced	1 cup	391
Marmalade	1 tablespoon	48
Molasses, blackstrap	1 tablespoon	43
Mushrooms	1 cup	25
Cooked mustard greens	1 cup	32
Green olives	10 olives	45
Ripe olives	10 olives	63
Green onions, chopped	1 tablespoon	2

Ingredient	Household Measure	kcals
Parsley, chopped	1 tablespoon	2
Roasted, salted peanuts	1 tablespoon	52
Cooked green peas	1 cup	114
Cooked peas and carrots	1 cup	85
Pecans	10 nuts	277
Fried perch	1 fillet	281
Pineapple, sweetened	4 chunks	52
Plums	10 plums	66
Radishes, sliced	1 cup	20
Raisins	1 tablespoon	26
Raspberries, black	1 cup	98
red	1 cup	70
Salmon	1 can, 7¾ ounces	447
Sardines	1 can, 3¾ ounces	330
Cooked spinach	1 cup	41
Strawberries	1 cup	55
Tomatoes	1 tomato	27
Tuna, chunk style	1 can, 6½ ounces	530
Turkey	3 ounces	162
Cooked turnip greens	1 cup	29
Cooked veal, diced	1 cup	329
Mixed vegetables, boiled	1 cup	116
White sauce	½ cup	247
Yogurt	1 cup	152

create a crepe

main dishes

Filling	Amount of Filling (each crepe)	Topping
Start with a sauce: White Sauce, Mornay Sauce, Veloute Sauce, etc.*		Thin sauce used in filling by adding whipping cream or sour cream
add:		or add:
cooked diced chicken, ham, seafood, or roast beef	¼ cup	grated cheese or chopped parsley
Asparagus or broccoli spears	4 spears	Hollandaise sauce and chopped watercress or grated cheese
Sautéed mushrooms and onions	¼ cup	Sautéed mushrooms or chopped parsley
Combination of poultry and vegetables or seafood and vegetables	¼ cup	Grated cheese, Sautéed mushrooms, or hollandaise sauce

desserts

Filling	Amount of Filling (each crepe)	Topping
Preserves: strawberry, apricot, etc.	2 tablespoons	Sour cream, whipped cream, soft custard, or vanilla ice cream
Orange marmalade	2 tablespoons	Whipped cream, hard sauce, or orange sherbet
Canned pie filling (cherry, blueberry, etc.)	¼ cup	Ice cream, whipped cream, or sour cream
Hot apple sauce	¼ cup	Caramel sauce, sugar-cinnamon mixture, or confectioner's sugar
Ice cream	¼ cup	Ice cream topping or sauce
Fresh fruit and sugar (strawberries, cherries, etc.)	¼ cup	Fruit toppings, whipped cream, nuts, or sugar
Canned fruit (sliced peaches, mandarin oranges, etc.)	¼ cup	Ice cream, nuts, or whipped cream

*See section on sauces

index